itchy

□□□□□

www.itchybristol.co.uk

© itchy Ltd
Globe Quay Globe Road Leeds LS11 5QG
t: 0113 246 0440 f: 0113 246 0550 e: all@itchymedia.co.uk
ISBN: 1-903753-15-5

City Manager	Kelly Halborg
Editorial Team	Simon Gray, Tamla Walker, Mike Waugh, Andrew Wood
Design	Matt Wood, Chris McNamara Maps by Steve Cox @ Crumb Eye Design
Photography	Clubbing section supplied by Bubblegum Magazine
Contributors	Alex Donohoe, Julie Guy, Alison Swann, Ed Guertin, Lesley Cunningham, Erica Groom, Jayne Carter Jess Dunton, Nicola Smith, Alex Sutherland, Estelle Burke, Su Lee, Alison Forrester.

THEY MUST PROMOTE
YOU. YOU'VE GOT
COMMITMENT.

contents

top fives & top tips

bristol 2002

Welcome to Bristol – the gateway to Wales – as some would have it, or the return to civilisation for most people. The capital of the South West, The World's Best City (GWR said it so it must be true) is blazing a trail with new architecture, business and finance but to be honest we don't really give a toss about that, we're concerned with spending the wealth, and slap me with a ferret if there's not enough places to do that. In its

second year itchy Bristol is gurning with new places. The last year has witnessed another explosion of bars, pubs and restaurants. This time next year there won't be a bank or warehouse that hasn't started flogging Sea Breezes.

■■ Areas

The town centre is split into smaller areas. The main shopping area is based around the soulless Broadmead centre but most of the better eating and drinking places are further towards the **Waterfront** area. If we lived in a more literal world **Park Street** would be called Beer Boulevard or maybe Lager Lane,

but we don't so it isn't. Park Street has more independent shops and bars and leads up to **Clifton Triangle**, which is more literally named and is home to some more decent boozers and bars and along with **Whiteladies Road** (just up from the triangle where the BBC is based) and **Clifton Village** (up the hill from the Triangle) is where the city's bundles of students tend to entertain themselves. The Village is home to The Clifton Suspension Bridge and Bristols' posh people; striking architecture and fancy restaurants to boot. Whiteladies Road is the destination of BBC luvvies and has enough bars and tapas to keep them in lunches for decades. **Gloucester Road**, **St Michael's Hill** and **Cotham** are the stomping ground of the more traditional drinkers, with some decent proper pubs and second-hand shops. **St Pauls** and **Montpellier** are the cities 'multicultural areas' as the council would put it. A bit rough around the edges but they're the home of Bristols' music scene with some wicked cafés and record shops and the atmosphere in some of the area's club nights is hard to beat.

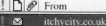

! 🗋 🖉 From	Subject
✉ itchycity.co.uk	Weekend offers to your inbox

■ ■ Two Hours in Bristol

Best get a move on. If you're on foot you'll be confined to the town centre and *Park Street* area. If you're after some retail therapy then you can choose from the *Broadmead shopping centre* if you're after the usual high street brands. Alternatively, take a trip up to *Park Street* for independent retailers. Now you'll have to head back down the hill with aching legs and on to the *Waterside*. itchy recommends the *Watershed Café Bar* for a cultural pit stop and bite to eat. Next take a few steps to the *Explore@Bristol* centre where the digital world comes to life or you can explore the tropical wonders of the rain forest through their state of the art planetarium. If you're not mesmerised by this place you may have room for a little more sight seeing in the *Industrial Museum* on *Wapping Road* where you can see several exhibits on the docking days of Bristol, but that's probably pushing it. There's so much to see and little time to do it in, so you'd best return we reckon.

■ ■ Two Days in Bristol

■ ■ A Blow Out Weekend

Accommodation – You want posh? Try the city centre *Marriot* on *College Green*. Around £45/night at weekends for absolute luxury.

Shopping – For all the big names that you'd expect in a city like this, you can't go wrong with *Broadmead* and the *Galleries*. But if you're after classy little boutiques and antiques shops, then scoot around *Clifton Arcade*. Also worth a peek are the shops around *Park Street*, especially for the young and stylish.

Attractions – *Explore@Bristol* (adult £6.50). See our entertainment section for more, but if this doesn't entertain you, you've got proper problems. Alternatively, there's always the *Bristol Zoo* (adults £8.40)

Eating – One of the best places to dine out has to be *Okra* (6 Chandos Road), near *Whiteladies* and *Clifton* which specialises in North African cuisine. If you're near town then blow your cash on a top class full on silver service meal at *Conrad at Jamesons* or *Upper Maudlin Street* – for a classy lunch it's surprisingly cheap, and the daytime express menu starts at £5.95. If you're a bit adventurous, try the new sushi bar in town, *Sukoshi* on *Frogmore Street*. Relax with a few bottles of bubbly, which start at £15 and rise to a cool £200.

Drinking – Depends on your taste really... or laid back sofa action try *Bar Humbug* on *Whiteladies Road*. Then there's vodka mayem at *Revolution* that's worth a go. Or the funky retro bar, *E-Shed* on *Canons Road* for something different. Cocktails? Easy – go to *Pulp*. Or maybe something more cultured? Try the *Arnolfi* bar on the *Waterfront*. Phew.

Clubbing – It's either clubbing proper or live music – check out our 'Best Nights For..' in the clubbing section or live music venues in the Entertainments section. The Bristol club scene covers all genres – cheese catered for at *Evolution, The Works* and *Creamrock* and style at *Creation, Level, The Lock* and the *Blue Mountain*.

■■ Cheapskates

Bristol on a budget eh? Try and get a car as places are spread out and taxis can set you back a bit – you have been warned.

Accommodation – The *Bristol Backpackers* at £12.50 a night should do the job.

Shopping – Window shopping on *Park Street* – you are on a budget remember?

Entertainment – The slightly off-puttingly named *Ginger Gallery* has free entry and you can admire real craftsmen at work. No? Then how about the *Ice Rink* just off *Park Street* will only set you back £4.60, which includes skate hire? Still not convinced? Well, there's always the free comedy at the *Bunch Of Grapes* pub on *Denmark street* on Sundays.

Eating – Dining on the cheap is easy, and one of the best places is the *Grillbar* in the city centre where you can get the best spit roast of your life (without cheating on your partner at least) for under a tenner. If the carnivore experience is too weighty then try out a pancake from the *Double Dutch Pancake* place on *Baldwin Street* – a meal for two including house wine will set you back a mere £21.65 (Oriental Pancakes), so go Dutch.

Drinking – Cultured drinking comes cheap in Bristol with a huge pub and bar scene. If you find yourself in *Park Street* duck into *Ha Ha Bar* for a refined bar experience. They do a great nibbles and munchies menu that is very reasonable. Moving on and up, what about the *Clifton/Whiteladies* area? *Henry J Beans* and *The Hophouse* stand out for cheap eats, but there's a whole host of options for grabbing a cheap bite.

Clubbing – Most clubs charge a high entry so if you're on a low budget it may be best to stick to a late night bar that doesn't charge. However, *The Fez* and *Po Na Na* are pretty reasonable on entry and cover most music genres.

restaurants

www.itchybristol.co.uk

■ ■ African

■ ■ Okra

6 Chandos Road, Redland (0117) 970 6078

A recently opened North African restaurant serving up Moorish and Berber cuisine. Not quite the African feel that you would expect although I'm not sure what exactly it was that I wanted to see... the odd camel and lots of sand maybe, although the inlaid brass, ivory and wood mirrors against the striking yellow walls go some way to setting the scene. The food, however, is something else – we're talking orgasm on a plate – and if you are a complete African cuisine virgin, the waiters will help you out without being obnoxious. As for cheap eats – try the three-course business lunch for a mere £12.50.

12-2.30 ('til 3 Sat only), 6-11 Mon-Sat 12-4, 6-11 Sun
Meal for two: £34.95 (Moorish Spiced Lambs Liver)

■ ■ Touareg

77 Whiteladies Road (0117) 904 4488

The flavour of France and Spain thousands of years ago, or so they say, although rest assured the food is totally fresh. The restaurant is set over two floors but it doesn't matter where you're seated as the Bedouin Room and the Tented Room are both stunningly decorated with wooden carvings, decorative tables and chairs, and there's even a water feature on the stairway. If romance is what you're after then Thursday evenings offer 'Casablanca' night with a pianist setting the scene. Sup on Moroccan mint tea and enjoy a truly authentic experience.

12-2, 6-11 Mon-Sun
Meal for two: £35.95 (Touareg Meze)

■ ■ ■ American/Pacific

■ ■ ■ The Firehouse Rotisserie

Anchor Sq, Harbourside (0117) 915 7323

Enjoy Southwest specials of spit roast chicken, Pacific grills, catfish or one of the famous LA brick-fired pizzas in this cavernous restaurant. The food is served from an open kitchen that, along with the wrought iron chandeliers, helps to create a relaxed rustic atmosphere. The owners spent years in Hollywood looking after the celebrities so they really know their stuff.

12pm-11pm Mon-Sun
Meal for two: £32.85 (1/2 rotisserie free range Texas spiced rubbed chicken)

■ ■ ■ TGI Fridays

Cribbs Causeway (0117) 959 1987

Everything in this place screams typically American – big, brash and in your face. Take the kids, order some burgers, down a few cocktails and stagger home by ten. Hardly what you'd call relaxing, but no-one said parenting was easy. Ideal for a family night out.

12-10.30 Sun-Thu, 12-11.30 Fri & Sat
Meal for two: £39.75 (Rib Eye Steak in Jack Daniels Sauce)

■ ■ ■ Australian

■ ■ ■ Melbournes

74 Park Street (0117) 922 6996

Good honest tucker in true Aussie style with no faffy, frilly bits attached. The walls are adorned with modern Australian and Aboriginal art, and it's a place popular with young people and families. The restaurant has a BYO policy with no corkage charge to complement the set price menu and renowned specials board. The sister restaurant in

Gloucester Road offers a different menu, specialising more in fresh fish and vegetarian cuisine, although the traditional kangaroo steak bounds onto the menu as well.

Park St 5pm-10.30pm Mon-Sat, closed Sun
Gloucester Road 6pm-10.30 Tue-Sat, closed Sun/Mon
Meal for two: £44.85 (Set 2 Course Dinner)

■ ■ ■ Belgian

■ ■ ■ Belgo

The Old Granary, Queen Charlotte Street (0117) 905 8000

Moules, frites, bieres – and not much else. A set lunch is on offer during the week with the promise that if it is not served within 12 minutes the food is free (why 12 minutes? I don't know). Interior-wise, we're talking sleek and modern with industrial steel and dark wood playing a large part. An enjoyable change, especially with the potent Belgian beers and the 25 flavoured schnapps on offer.

12-3, 5.30-10.30 Mon-Thu,
12-11.30 Fri & Sat, 12-10.30 Sun
Meal for two: £29.85 (Bucket of Mussels)

■ ■ Chinese/Oriental

■ ■ Budokan

31 Colston Street (0117) 914 1488

Budokan have certainly found the winning formula when it comes to cuisine. '98 saw the opening of the first, with the second restaurant opening in Feb 2001. It's been described as an 'Asian style fuelling station'. Pictures spring to mind of queues, utter confusion and a 'fill 'em up, get 'em out' mentality. In reality it's far different, and it's continually growing in popularity and receiving nominations for national awards. The dishes come from all over Asia and Japan, whilst the benches come with a guarantee to give you a numb arse and a sore back.

12-3, 5.30-12am Mon-Sat
Meal for two: £ 23.50 (Tempura of Chicken)

■ ■ Chi Chinese Cuisine

21 Regent Street (0117) 907 7840

Descend the stairs to be greeted with

smiles, served with smiles and given the bill with smiles – which is either utterly charming or incredibly annoying depending on what mood you're in. It all gets kind of infectious and if you see the beaming faces parading through Clifton Village at night you know exactly where they've been eating. The Early Bird Special (6-7.30) three course dinner for a mere £8 per person is particularly awesome.

12-2 Thu-Sat, 6-11.30 Mon-Sun
Meal for two: £28.90 (Set Meal)

■ ■ Dynasty

16a Thomas St (0117) 925 0888/3888

Think big. Bristol's largest Chinese restaurant has gone for the sophisticated look with a fully air-conditioned, cream walled, air hanger sized room set off with a shed load of huge paintings and Chinese decorations. No globiduous MSG here. Instead, it specialises in Peking and Szechuan cuisine with an extensive menu as well as a wide range of fresh seafood, all adding to the confusion of why on earth they need to resort to a karaoke system. I mean, the food's bloody great but will someone shove a pancake roll into that bloke on table 9's mouth. Have these people no shame?

12 pm-11.30 pm Mon-Sun
Meal for two: £47.95 (Three course set meal)

■ ■ New World

Unit 1 Unite House, Frogmore Street (0117) 929 3288

Bristol's very own Oriental karaoke buffet restaurant. What a combination. The Japanese certainly have a lot to answer for. Opening as the book was going to print, they've opted for a modern and certainly eye-catching style of décor. The buffet offers over forty dishes to choose from, all for a mere £13, which is not bad value at all, even taking into consideration that the bloke who was sitting at table 9 at Dynasty last night has just showed up and is heading for the mic.

12-2.30, 6-11 Sun-Thu, 12-2.30,
6-12 Fri & Sat
Meal for two: £35 (Buffet)

■■■ British

■■■ Deason's Restaurant

43 Whiteladies Road (0117) 973 6230

Sharp, sophisticated and contemporary dining has come to Bristol in the form of Deasons. After a successful year on the

Whiteladies strip, the gourmet talents of head chef, Jason Deason, have put this independent eatery on the kudos list in top eating circles. Injecting innovation and developing new flavours in each menu created is top on the agenda for this chap and it's this quality of service that sets this place apart from most. The restaurant evokes a similar tone with art displayed from local artists on the walls, candlelit tables, fine glassware and a crisp, fresh feel to the place. Outside seating has been added for alfresco dining on warm summer nights (rare) and a bar at the entrance make this a pleasant location for the discerning eater who relishes new discoveries. Stop me if I'm gushing... we like it.

12-2.30, Mon-Sat, 6.30-10 Mon-Thu,
6.30-10.30 Fri & Sat, 12-3 Sun
Meal for two: £41.75 (Two Courses)

■■■ Grillbar

The Haymarket, Town Centre
(0117) 910 0666

"Come and eat and drink like there's no tomorrow". I took their advice and I did. Three courses later, having stuffed my face like a force-fed turkey at Christmas I still had enough money left to drink myself into obvlivion. Grillbar boast no frills food at affordable prices, and with lunch from £5.50 and dinner from £7.50 you can't argue. Plenty of sofas to lounge around in after your gargantuan meal and vat-full of booze. Recommended.

Mon-Fri 12-10.30, Sat 12-11, Sun 12-10.30
Meal for two: £42 ('Sharing Plate' – a bit of everything [not literally])

■■■ Hullaballoos

85 Park Street (0117) 907 7540/46
46 Whiteladies Road (0117) 923 9212

A couple of British/European stylised restaurants that serve the masses well. Expect booth style seating and scatter tables plonked amidst enough plants to rival a jungle . Hullaballoos is equally suitable for large groups or an intimate dinner date. Friendly

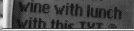

itchy sms @
www.itchybristol.co.uk

Come and Eat and Drink

like there's no tomorrow

At Grillbar you can enjoy unpretentious, affordable food and drink that's rustled up not dressed up. Grillbar is about eating and drinking like there's no tomorrow.

Grillbar's mouthwatering selection of freshly chargrilled food starts from just £5.50 for lunch and £7.50 for dinner.

grillbar

The Haymarket.
Bristol.
Tel: 01179 100 66

service and silver service efficiency, so it helps if you know which way the cutlery works (it's also considered very bad form to drink the finger bowl). Meals are a mix of light bites, steaks, salads and some decent meat and veggie dishes. And they've got a BYO policy. Great value.

12-2.15 & 6 'til late Mon-Sat, 12-3.30, 6 'til late Sun
Meal for two: £30 (Three course meal). BYO.

■ ■ ■ Markwicks Restaurant
43 Corn Street (0117) 926 2658

Classy, real classy. A marble staircase leads you to a restaurant that resembles a stately home. It's all a bit bleedin' posh, so I was understandably nervous about eating here. And besides, my expense account had been all but used up on the bars so in the interests of providing you lot with a decent review, I was forced to humiliate myself by standing and drooling by table 8 and asking a lovely young couple exactly how good the food was. To their credit, they put up with me for a good twenty minutes before politely suggesting that I sod off. With wood-panelled walls, separate dining booths and racks of fine wines on display, you know they're gonna bill your arse at the end of the night. The menu changes regularly and is full of fresh fish, meat and game and prices are chokingly high, but worth every penny according to Ava and Dan on table 8. I should jolly well hope so at prices like that.

12-2, 7-10 Mon-Fri, 7-10 Sat
Meal for two: £46.50 (Rack of Lamb with Garlic Sauce)

■ ■ ■ Caribbean

■ ■ ■ Café Cariba
45 Jamaica Street (0117) 944 2348

More a café than a restaurant but for the real Caribbean experience look no further. Aptly located on Jamaica Street, this friendly café is the business. With red, yellow and green walls and makeshift back garden seating, you get to feel you're actually in Jamaica and are just waiting for Bob Marley to cruise on by... the fact that he's been dead for over 20 years and the weather's shitty and that bastard bus on the High Street has just driven straight through a puddle and soaked you from head to toe shouldn't distract you from this fantasy in the least. The menu is typically Jamaican with authentic curried meat or vegetarian patties and jerk chicken sandwiches. It's not a licensed café, so none of your Malibu moments found in here. However, they do have a large list of fruit drinks such as their pineapple punch and fruit nectar drinks all under £1.50. Bargain.

9am-7pm Mon-Sun
Meal for two: £10.50 (Ackee and Saltfish Meal & Guinness Punch)

■ ■ ■ Dutch

■ ■ ■ Double Dutch Pancakes
45-47 Baldwin Street (0117) 929 0433

Go Dutch. Pancakes, pancakes and more pancakes. The Dutch version of a tortilla wrap really, with virtually any filling conceivable. Have it hot or cold, sweet or savoury (no weed pancakes on the menu – it's not

koko.com

that Dutch). Break the monotony with a waffle or two or some Dutch lager, but that's about exciting as it gets. An altogether strange and unfulfilling experience – a bit like that 'adventure' you had when you visited Amsterdam.

12-3, 6-11 Mon-Fri, 12-12 Sat
Meal for two: £21.65 (Oriental Pancake)

■■■ French

■■■ Chez Gérard
37-39 Corn Street (0117) 917 0490

So very, very French, but thankfully without the stereotypical onions and garlic hanging from the walls. Don't be put off by the castle-like exterior, as the inside has all of the style and intimacy you'd expect from such a French affair. It's almost like a classier rendition of the Orient Express with brown leather booth seating, glass partitions and a tiled black and white floor creating a contemporary feel. Bottles of wine from the extensive wine list (all exclusively French of course) are displayed in glass cabinets on the wall. The café menu served from 11am-6pm offers quick and light bites or you can choose from the lunchtime set menu of 2 courses for £10.95. The à la carte menu has a selection of meat, grills, fish and vegetarian dishes. Set menus start at £15.95 with the option of four courses for an extra £3.95. And when it's not raining you can go all continental and grab a seat on the terrace. There are few reasons to doubt their claim of being the best this side of Paris.

12pm-11pm Mon-Sat
Meal for two: £30.50 (Roasted Pork Fillet on Savoy Cabbage with Cider and Apple Jus)

■■■ Glass Boat
Welshback (0117) 929 0704

If you're looking for a place to take that special person in your life, then look no further. If romance is on your menu then this is just the place. The elegance of the Glass Boat with views over the river make this the perfect place to impress. Students forget it; the food is just too good for you and way out of your price range, and what's more, they don't like you here. Watch the sun rise over a champagne breakfast or watch it set over dinner or do both (although they may chuck you out in between). Wine tastings and live jazz evenings are regularly held so sit back, leave your worries behind and watch the world go by (that is, until the bill arrives).

7am-10.15am, 12-2.15, 6.30 'til late Mon-Fri, 6.30pm-12.30am Sat
Meal for two: £36.90 (Seared Grey Mullet)

■■■ Ma Provence
2 Upper Byron Pl. Clifton (0117) 926 8314

This place is worth searching out (just off the Clifton Triangle) if you want quality French cuisine at an affordable price. Once sampled you're likely to return. Why?

Because it's cheap and it's good. Simple. Absolutely adored by those who really recognise and appreciate good food.
11.30-2.30 Mon-Fri, 6.30-11 Mon-Sat
Meal for two: £38.40 (Veal Kidneys with Pomme Paillasson)

■ ■ ■ Conrad at Jamesons
30 Upper Maudlin St (0117) 927 6565
The menu is broadly English and French with a few Mediterranean and Eastern hints, and that's the nearest to pigeon holing this place as you'll get. The vegetarian selection and the seafood specialities should put this place firmly near the top of your 'places I must visit' list. Perfect for business lunches or dinner with your aunt.
12-12 Mon-Sun
Meal for two: £33.95 (Warm Leek and Cheese Tart)

■ ■ Greek

■ ■ ■ Bouboulina's
9 Portland Street (0117) 973 1192

Offers a relaxed Greek style of eating, which on those rare sunny days can be captured by sitting outside surrounded by hanging baskets. The restaurant itself is split into various rooms and levels, so for that inti-

mate dinner date head for a quiet alcove whilst the more rowdy customer who wants to fling a few plates around (please ask) can take over a room or two. A daily lunch menu is available between 12 and 4 as well as the à la carte, individual mezze or mezebes (set) menus in the evenings. Vegetarians and vegans are well catered for along with those who have special dietary requirements. Don't expect too many chemicals or GM additives as much of the ingredients are organic.

5-11 Mon, 12-11 Tue-Sat, 12-9 Sun
Meal for two: £36.85 (Klephtiko)

■ ■ ■ Indian

■ ■ ■ The One Stop Thali Café
12a York St, Montpellier (0117) 942 6687
Situated on a street corner, this tiny restaurant is based on the roadside cafes of India – dhabas. The 'thalis', a combination of dishes, which complement each other, served up on a steel plate, provide a cheap and tasty meal – and an entire meal consisting of six dishes can cost as little as £6. It's perfect for small parties or horrendously skint people and is also proving amongst local meatless people who go for the vegetarian Sunday lunch. A chilled, eclectic, mellow atmosphere pervades and the musicians who stop off here enhance that vibe, so pitch a tent, chain yourself to a tree and enjoy.

11am-4.30pm, 6-11.30pm Tue-Sun
Meal for two: £20 (Thalis – rice, salad,
yoghurt, vegetable & lentil selection)

■ ■ ■ Rajdoot Tandoori
83 Park Street (0117) 926 8033

Rajdoot is part of a small chain with restaurants in Birmingham, Manchester and wait for it... Fuengirola on the Costa Del Sol. The white and orange exterior isn't the most inviting, and once inside you're greeted by the traditional wooden décor, gaudy carpets and of course the odd elephant or two. An à la carte menu is available every evening with 25% discount between 6.30-7.30 Sun-Thu. The four course business lunch is only £7.95 Mon-Fri between 12 and 2.

12-2.15, 6-11.30 Mon-Sat, 6-11 Sun
Meal for two: £26.75 (Makhan Chicken)

■ ■ ■ Rajpoot
52 Upper Belgrave Road, Clifton
(0117) 973 3515
This family run Indian restaurant set in a Georgian house overlooking the Downs smacks of elegance, from the wooden chairs to the tasteful yellow walls with their large

LOOK AT HIM, POMPOUS IDIOT.

s and colourful artwork. Forget your
nd vindaloo as what you will get is
tional authentic Indian cuisine served
classy surroundings. Refinement is the
of the day so no pissed up lager louts
e, thank you very much.

30, 6-11 Mon-Sat
for two: £ 31.95 (Tikka Massala)

■ International

■ Naranjas Fusion Brasserie
sley Road (0117) 973 4892

not raining, sit outside Naranjas and
nd you're in a more exotic part of
e; if it's raining (which it will be), then
h your back to the window and enjoy
credibly varied and lovingly prepared
of Eastern and Western dishes. You
ven enter a different time zone and
breakfast anytime between 8am and
and lunch up until 7.30pm. Perfect for
os or people with jetlag.

9pm Mon-Sat, 9am-5pm Sun
for two: £36.85 (Two course set menu)

■ Tico Tico Restaurant
na Vale Road (0117) 923 8700

le a promise to myself that I would
use the word 'fusion' in a restaurant
v. I also promised to give up smoking
eek and I failed at that too. Tico Tico
ade for the word 'fusion' – to talk about
co and omit the word 'fusion' would be
So before I start, I would like to formal-
logise for the excessive use of the word

'fusion' in the following review. Thank you.
Read on. Tico Tico offers a MediterrAsian
fusion style of cooking – weird sounding, I
know, but it somehow works. None of our
subtle flavours here. The fusion of flavours is
about as subtle as the fusion of particles in
an atom bomb – guaranteed to get your
taste buds exploding. Decorated in welcoming yellow, you are guaranteed a friendly
atmosphere and a warm welcome.
Courtyard dining adds to the whole fusion
experience. Except when it's raining. And
then you'll just get wet. Obviously.

7-10.30 Tue-Sat
Meal for two: £38.85 (Set 2 course dinner)

top 5...
To Impress

1.	Touareg
2.	Glassboat
3.	Chez Gérard
4.	Budokan
5.	Ma Provence

▨ ■ Italian

▨ ■ Planet Pizza
83 Whiteladies Road (0117) 907 7112

Not the over-rated, over-hyped American
tack you might expect from the name.
Instead, a small funky place set amongst the
bars and eateries of the Whiteladies strip.
The bright orange exterior will catch your

**TOO BUSY DIGESTING HIS FOUR HOURS
LUNCH TO LISTEN TO YOU**

eye and prepare to be dazzled by the brightly coloured walls and abstract art inside. A place to sit back and relax with the morning papers, and also a place to start your night. The pizzas are aptly named after planets but fortunately with little resemblance – Planet Earth is a healthy veggie and mozzarella combination as opposed to a polluted mess. A cosmic experience you could say – if you were a very sad, lonely individual anyway.

11-11 Mon-Sat, 11-10.30 Sun
Meal for two: £29.45 (Planet Earth Veggie Pizza)

■ ■ ■ San Carlo
44 Corn Street (0117) 922 6586

In true Italian style, San Carlo is sophisticated, contemporary and stylish. Everything has a clean crisp look, from the tablecloths to the waiters that bustle around. Olympic style torches welcome you at the entrance whilst the blue lighting, mirrored walls and glass features cause everything to shimmer and shine. The service is snappy from the ever attentive staff, who at times appear to

out number the clientele. Despite the the food remains authentic and top n with an extensive menu offering anyt from pasta, pizzas and salads to seafood meat dishes. A plush Italian experie worth every penny.

7-11 Mon-Sun
Meal for two: £28.45 (Pan Fried Veal ir Lemon and White Wine Sauce)

■ ■ ■ Sergios
Frog Lane (0117) 929 1413

Bristol's first BYO Italian – the wine tha the Italians are provided. Warm undert of Italy set in the old style buildings of Lane. Two rooms with as many ta crammed together as possible for that intimate feeling. Expect colourful ye napkins stuffed in glasses, chalk bc announcing specials of the day, along Italian slogans and paintings. Dare I s even better than Mama can cook it. Ide a post theatre meal.

12pm-2.15pm, 5.45pm-11pm Mon-Fri,
5.45pm-11pm Sat, closed Sun
Meal for two: £ 21 (Duck Breast in Ora Balsamic Sauce), corkage charge 95p

WELL, DIGEST THIS!

■ Japanese

■ Azuma

yron Place, Triangle South, Clifton
17) 927 6864

authentic Japanese restaurant has been
ed amongst the eight best in the coun-
A small but modern venue that manages
reate a relaxed atmosphere without the
nour and fuss of its counterparts. As a
plement to your meal, sit back and
y traditional sake or Japanese lager.
ions are generous and great value for
ey, so if it's true Japanese food you want
look no further. Better still, there's not a
oke machine in sight.

0-2.30, 7.30 'til late
for two: £40.90 (Teriyaki Beef)

■ Sukoshi

e House, Frogmore St (0117) 927 6003
ainly not for the faint hearted. Don't get
wrong, the food's top notch but the
es of shrieks and squeals reverberate
nd the room as customers are
ralled (or was it repulsed) by the adven-
us dishes served up. The restaurant
s itself on its authentic Japanese dishes

and sushi selection. Champagne – yes please
– just a small matter of thirty to choose from
ranging in price from around £15 to a cool
£220. The interior is breathtaking with the
two stone water walls adding to the traditional wood, stone water thingy (can you tell
I know my stuff?). A must for those of you
feeling adventurous or who want to try
something just that little bit different.

11am-12am Mon-Sun
Meal for two: £26.85 (Teriyaki Tuna)

■ ■ Lebanese/Moroccan

■ ■ Sands

Queens Road (0117) 973 9734
The staff are incredibly helpful here, which is
useful as the menu is full of names designed
to tie your tongue in knots. Ask about the
Arabian theme nights at £14.95 per person
complete with belly dancer (that's shared –
not per person). The menu is varied including hot and cold mezze starting at £14.95,
and also containing an extensive vegetarian
selection. And before you ask, no, it's not a
bong, it's a Shisha, and yes, only sweet tobacco flavoured with honey and apple is available, nothing else. Damn.

11.30am-2.30pm, 6pm-11pm Mon-Sun
Meal for two: £42.75 (Special mezza for 2)

■ ■ Taste of Morocco

180 Gloucester Road (0117) 907 4073
Visit and savour the flavours of the Med
shores, the High Atlas, the Sahara and more
in this fully licensed restaurant on

Gloucester Road. As with all eateries, they promise the finest of ingredients, traditional cuisine and a new experience – and believe me they've actually managed to live up to their word. Not the type of place that would automatically spring to mind for a night out, but definitely worth a shot.

6-11 Sun-Thu, 6-11.30 Fri & Sat
Meal for two: £24.70 (Moroccan Lamb)

■ ■ Mexican/South American

■ ■ Casa Caramba
1 Regent Street (0117) 974 3793
You surely can't miss the brightly coloured orange and blue exterior, but just in case you do, the sweet smell of spices are there to tempt you inside. Spread across three levels; for the intimate dinner outing try the top floor; you can watch the world go by or make the ex feel jealous by sitting your new bird on the middle floor next to the large windows. Larger parties and short people (the ceilings are low in the back) can take over the downstairs. Either way, you're faced with bold, bright colours, Mexican memorabilia and generous portions.

7-10 Sun & Mon, 7-10.30 Tues-Thu,
6.30-11 Fri & Sat
Meal for two: £28.45 (Seafood Wrap)

■ ■ Las Iguanas
10 St. Nicholas Street (0117) 927 6233
Latin American and Spanish influenced fo amidst acid inspired décor and neck achi works of art in the form of light shades careful). From the crop of 'Latino' restaura that have emerged over the recent ye this is probably the best of the bunch. indigestion-sized portions set a challenge get through three courses. Avoid if you d like latin jazz or if you think that chic gravy is too extravagant. Like all of 'Iguanas' dotted about Bristol they're b brash, and dish out a menu of cocktails are positively lethal. Happy hour runs Sat and all day Monday from 5pm-7.30p

Mon-Thu 12-3pm, 5-11pm, Fri 12-3
5-11.30pm, Sat 12-11.30pm, Sun-close
Meal for two: £ 25.50 (Chimichanga's)

■ ■ Tequila Max
109 Whiteladies Road (0117) 946 614
Who is this Max guy and why can't I m him – I'm sure my mum'd hate him, bu certainly throws an excellent party. Fo authenticity – although the fake Mex tack on the walls could fool you (especia you were really pissed). The portions have you looking like the pot-be Mexican above the door. The place is us packed out with people taking advanta happy hour between 5 and 7 when coc are 2-4-1. This sets the scene for the re the evening – especially when the stud are in town. Tequila Max is certain appropriate name – the food is just an a bonus, so go, sample and stumble hom

12-2.30 Mon-Fri, 5-11 Sun-Thu, 5-12 F
Sat, 5-10.30 Sun
Meal for two: £29.85 (Chicken Fajitas,

▪ ▪ Seafood

▪ ▪ Fishworks Seafood Café and Fish Market

28 Whiteladies Road (0117) 974 4433

You go up to the counter, pick the fish you want, and then watch it fry. So you can check they don't spit in your food.

11am-11pm Tue-Sat
Meal for two: £38 (Wood Grilled Tuna with Red Onion and Pine Nut Relish)

▪ ▪ Fishers Restaurant

35 Princess Victoria Street, Clifton Village (0117) 974 7044

With BSE and foot and mouth hogging the headlines, the masses are turning to fish – which is reasonable as they have no feet and little brain so until the next scare they seem to be okay. The menu changes daily to reflect the night's catch and there's usually shark and barracuda on offer. For the knotted hanky type amongst you rest assured, there are also the English favourites of had-dock and chips with mushy peas, skate and Dover sole. A simple and in no way preten-tious kinda place.

12-2.30, 6-10.30 Tue-Sat, 12-4 Sun
Meal for two: £39.45 (Whole Lemon Sole)

▪ ▪ Red Snapper

Chandos Rd, Redland (0117) 973 7999

Award-winning restaurant with an emphasis on fresh and unusual fish. The menu changes regularly, reflecting the season. The overwhelming success of the restaurant has tempted it to expand, doubling the num-ber of tables and creating an outside eating area making it ideal for all occasions (except for when it's raining, snowing, windy, foggy or very cold).

12-2 Tue-Sat, 7.30-10 Mon-Thu, 7-10 Fri and Sat, 1-3 Sun
Meal for two: £42.50 (Red Snapper)Meal for two: £27.85 (Paella de Marisco)

▪ ▪ Thai

▪ ▪ Thai Classic

87 Whiteladies Road (0117) 973 8930

Not quite so classic now, and in need of a revamp. The staff are 100% Thai and prove it by their grasp of the English language, so Thai phrase books at the ready. To be on the safe side, use the universal language of point at the menu and smile. The food ain't half bad though. A special lunch of two courses for £6 is on offer and can be washed down with a selection of French wines – strange I know, but it was too painful to ask.

12-2.30, 5.30-11.30 Mon-Sun
Meal for two: £26.85 (Ped Tord Grob – crispy duck)

bars

www.itchybristol.co.uk

■ ■ All Bar One
Corn Street (0117) 9468751

You've seen one, you've seen 'em all. That' kinda the point – that whenever you're awa from home you can find a nice familiar A Bar One with the usual wooden dinin tables, big clocks and daily newspapers. No exactly riveting stuff, but if you're looking fo no atmosphere and a reasonable Chardonna to down with your parents then this plac fits the bill. Over 21s only.

Mon-Sat 12-11, Sun closed
Meal for two: £27.70 (Lamb Steak & Basil Mash)

■ ■ Arc Bar
Broad Street (0117) 922 6456

The original 'geek chic' bar, Arc's individu sense of style is now being copied by othe all over the city; they don't pull it off course, as there is only one Arc, and refusal to conform is what attracts t crowds. It's hidden away, so you'll have work to find it, but when you get the expect basic metal chairs in a cave settin an open fire, barmen who look like comp er technicians, wild DJs and some of the b live music in the city. Better still, it's bei extended to include a media/arts spa which will house local talent. Have we no ing bad to say about the place? No. Sorry

Tue-Thu 12-3am, Fri 12-2am, Sat 7-2am, Sun-6-12.30am
Meal for two: £14 (Fabulous Pizza)

■ ■ Bar Essential
54 Queen Charlotte St. (0117) 925 483

A hop, skip and a jump to the harboursid

EEL THE
RESENCE

PATRICIA GRANT.
FASHION DESIGNER

A MELLOW MIX OF SPIRIT AND SOUL.
THAT FLAVOURS WHATEVER IT TOUCHES.

* Try it with lemonade and ice after dancing.

and that's what you might feel like doing after being in this bar for a night. Somewhat lacking in ambience and tradition with brash colours and Neanderthal punters who like to 'ave it large with their mates. Their drink promos are aimed at the student market at the beginning of the week with drinking games such as toss the coin, roll the dice as well as card games. The things we'll do for cheap booze, eh?

Mon-Thu 12-11pm, Fri 12-1am,
Sat 6pm-1am, Sunday – closed
Meal For Two: £17.45 (Homemade Burger
& Jacket Potato)

■ ■ Bar Latino
12 Crusader House, St Stephens Street
(0117) 909 0212

Basement bar/club, with a rustic Mediterranean theme. There's a separate seating and dancefloor area, which is small and intimate rather than tiny and cramped. The popular Empathy tech and progressive house night kicks the weekend into shape with resident DJ Stuart Wilkinson 'til 3am on Thursdays with weekly guests. Other nights include 'Kung Fu disco' – a mish-mash of hip hop and electro beats on Monday or trance

on Tuesday with 'Bizarre'. The 'Funky Onion' outfit take up alternate Saturday slots with Junior 95 and the 'Illicit' crew give you that Friday feeling with uplifting house and US garage 'til the early hours.

No dress code any night of the week.
Mon-Fri 5-3am, Sat 8-3am, Sun 8-3am

■ ■ Brooklyn Bar
Corn Street (0117) 927 9193

Home to Bristol's trendy crew, so Edward regulars had better stay away. Sofas and low tables adorn the front room, which get busy throughout the day, mainly because it's popular, but also because it's on the small side. If you need to spread out though, there's two more floors to work your way around. The first floor has DJs pumping out tunes throughout the week, whilst the cocktail bar on the top floor is the place to welcome in the midnight hours once the doors open after 9pm. Superb any time of the day and the perfect place to avoid the chain bar tat that litters the town centre. If that's not enough, it's all free. Nice one.

Mon-Fri 12-1am, Thu-Sat 12-2am,
Sun 4-11pm

■ ■ Edwards
7-9 Baldwin Street (0117) 930 4370

Edwards are known up and down the country for being crap, and this one's no different. Best avoided altogether, unless of course you are a bit of a twat with a craving for alcopops.

Mon-Tue 10am-11pm, Wed 10am-12am,
Thu-Sat 10am-1am, Sun 12pm-12.30am
Meal For Two: £20 (Hickory Chicken)

■ ■ Grillbar

The Haymarket, Town Centre
(0117) 910 0666

With so many poncey bars kicking about Bristol it's refreshing to see a bar that's not afraid to say what it does plain and simple. Drink like there's no tomorrow, eat like a pig and collapse on a sofa – you're in the Grillbar. Inside it's all sleek corners, squidgy sofas, wooden tables and chairs. You can stop off any time of day for a casual drink in the bar downstairs or eat 'til you burst upstairs. Either way, you can't escape the mouth-watering smell of sizzling meat and vegetables coming from the open plan kitchens. Splendid.

Mon-Sat 11am-11.00pm, Sun 12-10.30pm
(bar times only)
Meal for two: £24 (Spit Roast Chicken)

■ ■ Mud Dock

The Grove (0117) 934 9734

A preacher in 17th century Baltimore described bicycles as diabolical devices of the demon of darkness, but even he might warm to them in here. With a cycle shop downstairs and café upstairs, you've reached the Mud Dock. Open daily to the masses, there's a small decked area to soak up the rays on those rare sunny days or you can chill out inside with laid back funky tunes and tapas to nibble on. DJs take regular slots over the weekend playing funky sets, so get on your two-wheeled contraption and pull into the Mud Dock.

Mon 11am-6pm, Tue-Sat 11am-11pm,
Sun 10-10.30pm
Meal For Two: £32.50 (Sea bass with Swiss Chard)

■ ■ The Prom Music Cafébar

26 The Promenade, Gloucester Road
(0117) 942 7319

Gloucester Road is generally overlooked as it's way off the beaten track. The Prom Bar, however, sticks out a mile, decorated, as it is, in bright green, orange and black. Open 'til 11pm, it's not your average 'lets pile in and get pissed bar'; it's more of a 'stop off, have a bite to eat, relax, and listen to some decent bands at night, bar'. Nightly entertainment is free during the week with every music genre covered from jazz to reggae. There's even a pop quiz on Tuesday that'll set you back a pound. The emphasis on quality is also present in the food menu with a reasonably priced menu. Inside, the venue is split into three areas: a bar, a dancefloor and stage area, and a select no-smoking area. On bright days you can grab a table outside. And if you're partial to a bit of meat and veg, check out the Sunday lunch at just £4.95.

Mon-Sat 10am-11pm, Sun 10am-10.30pm
Meal For Two: £14.95 (Chicken Enchilladas)

■ ■ ■ Pulp

10 St Nicholas Street (0117) 930 4466

Be impressed. No, be very impressed. Not only does this basement bar sport some of the funkiest décor in the city and bring in top DJs at the weekends, it also turns out the best French martinis that you're ever likely to taste. Comfy sofas are dotted around the place, but leave those for the suits and grab yourself a stool at the bar. From here, girls can drool into their Manhattans as they watch the rather gorgeous barmen crushing limes and ice with big sticks. It's incredibly erotic – really... especially after a few drinks. No, it's not sad; cheap thrills aren't easy to come by in the politically correct 21st century. Are you blokes feeling left out? Let's cut to the chase

– this place is full of hot, horny women, so you're pretty much sorted on that score. Failing that, you could always get Smiley, the barman (no, we never did find out his real name) to line up the tequilas for a night that will be so memorable you'll be getting flashbacks in years to come.

Mon-Sat 5pm-1am
Meal for two: £18.00 (Nachos & Dips)

■ ■ ■ Revolution

The Old Fish Market, St. Nicholas Street (0117) 930 4335

A grandiose Russian influenced bar and munchery. In this country we still tend to think of Russia as a place full of never-ending bread queues and Stalinist purges. We shouldn't be so righteous and just accept that it's really just a mafia-controlled third world country. We should also thank them for one of the greatest drinks ever known to man – vodka. Revolution serve the stuff by the bucketload, and in numerous flavours. You should try out the pitcher options – what about the 'Stout Russian' for £11.50? Or you can keep it simple with a long drink of infused vodka on ice. However, if you're anything like me you'll always be up for the shot stick challenge, six shots of vodka for £7. Just make sure you allow plenty of time the following day to recover.

Mon-Sat 12-2am, Sun 12-12.30am
Meal for two: £14.50 (Baby Back Ribs & BBQ sauce – evening menu)

■ ■ ■ Slug and Lettuce

26-28 Nicholas Street (0117) 929 0313

Offering the same old tosh that most chain bars dish up – so expect simple, clean interiors, lots of ice-cream coloured walls and overpriced drinks. Yes, it fits in perfectly with the usual insipid atmosphere that is conjured up when you think chain.

Mon-Fri 11-11pm, Sat-Sun 12-10.30pm
Meal for two: £23.50 (Cajun Spiced Chicken Burger)

■■ Tantric Jazz
39-41 St Nicholas Street (0117) 940 2304
Tantric Jazz is one of those 'must see' places that often get overlooked, but it's certainly worth checking out. There's a Bohemian feel to the place and, despite the oddly patterned tablecloths and plain decor, it fills up impressively with arty, alternative types and beautiful people. Serving up tasty Middle Eastern/North African cuisine and some great musical talent, it's a real winner. Definitely one to put on your list.
Mon-Sat 5-11pm, Sun 6-11.30pm
Meal for two: £28.50 (Aromatic Chicken)

■■ Welsh Back

■■ Belgo Bar
Downstairs in the Old Granary, Queen Charlotte Street (0117) 905 8000
Belgo oozes chic sophistication without being up its own arse – how refreshing. Whether you want to kick back or knees up, this place will serve the purpose. If you're up for it there's always the 32 shot fruity schnapps sticks... though you'd best have an ambulance standing by in case you actually manage to finish the mammoth task.

Doesn't appeal? Well, you'll just have to pick from the 101 different beers instead. A fantastic bar that packs a punch – not literally, that'd be the schnapps.
Mon-Wed 5pm-11pm, Thu-Sat 5pm-1am, Sun – closed
Meal for two: £32.95 (Spicy Thai Curry)

■■ Bar Med
King Street (0117) 904 0061
Classy and sophisticated it ain't. It may be next to the Waterfront, but this is more Margate than Monte Carlo. Packed with teenage tartlets (who are over eighteen, honest guv... no really, they are eighteen, check out the dodgy ID cards if you don't believe me) and male saddos (who are under forty, honest guv... no really, they're still in their prime and would never resort to dying their greying hair, check out their extensive knowledge of popular music if you don't believe me), it's a bit of a shit pit. A giant tackfest with drinks at pocket money prices and a gaggle of slappers always chucking up in the bogs. Nice.
Mon-Thu 11-11, Fri- Sat 11am-2am, Sun 11-10.30pm
Meal for two: £26.85 (Paella)

■■ Waterfront

■■ Arnolfini Bar
16 Narrow Quay (0117) 927 9330
It's hard to believe, but there is such a thing as cultured drinking. No, really. Check out Arnolfini if you think I'm having you on; you'll be blown away with the Scandinavian

DRINK VODKA OR ELSE.

AND I WOULDN'T ARGUE IF I WERE YOU. 100 WAYS TO DRINK VODKA INCLUDING 30 UNIQUE FLAVOURS AND INFUSIONS. LATE NIGHT LOUNGIN' UNTIL 2AM ON THURSDAY, FRIDAY AND SATURDAY. FREE ADMISSION. HIP HOP/FUNKY BREAKS/R AND B/SOUL. VODKA HEAVEN IS REVOLUTION IS VODKA HEAVEN.

RƎVOLUTION

style and subtle ambience. So how have they managed to pull it off? Well, it's all been snazzed up by top architect David Chipperfield and artist Bruce McLean. It's one bar in town that refuses to entice the inebriated folk through the doors and gratefully shuns the beating drum anthems that are oh so popular across the water. If you're looking to get totally plastered and hoping for a quick fumble with your best mate's bird – avoid and stick to the chain bars, but for those with a little grey matter it comes highly recommended.

Mon-Sat 10am-11pm, 12-10.30 Sun
Meal for two: £19.70 (Med Meal)

■ ■ Chicago Rock Café
The Waterfront, Canons Road
(0117) 929 1361

So shit it hurts. Female divorcees by the bucketload and blokes who are looking to get laid without paying for it for once. In short, we're talking crumblies pick-up joint complete with pre-eighties playlist, glittering discoball and small dancefloor. Over 21s only – you're telling me.

Mon-Sat 11.30am-2am, Sun 12-12am
Lunch menu meal deal £14.75

■ ■ E – Shed
Canons Road (0117) 907 4287

Red, red, red all the way – from the walls to the sofas. You might be fooled into thinking you're in "Kubrick's 2001". The E-Shed stands out bold 'n' funky against the otherwise more neutral tones of the Waterfront. A lively pre-club bar or hang out that has a superb

cocktail list and one of the few places in Bristol that sells Absinthe by the bucketload. With a hot line up of nightly entertainment from laid-back funk, soul and hip-hop grooves to progressive house (Fridays) and UK garage (Saturdays). This place rocks.

Mon-Sat 12pm-2am, Sun 12pm-12.30am
Falafels & Garnish £17.85

■ ■ Pitcher & Piano
V Shed, Canons Road, Bristol
(0117) 929 9652

This place is bloody massive. Think jumbo-jet hanger size and you'll have an idea of the scale we're talking about. Three floors to get lost in and a silly amount of seating, which makes the place look like more of a furniture store than a bar – so come and lounge, take over the place, they won't mind as long as you buy something. Thirty-somethings tend to gather downstairs, whilst upstairs is always banging with whipper-snappers partying away 'til the early hours.

Mon-Thu 12pm-11pm, Fri-Sat 12pm-12am, Sun 12pm-10.30pm.
Meal for two: £28.00 (Spiced Moroccan lamb shank)

■ ■ ■ Torches Café/Bar
Canons Road, The Waterfront
(0117) 922 0382

Torches is the pre-club bar for Evolution next door. It's busy – all the time – and the perfect place to relax over a white wine spritzer with your cousin. No – I lie. It is busy, but it's also loud and packed with an up-for-it crowd. There's a fair amount of female talent in miniscule lycra club gear to be found here if you're looking to pull, whilst the blokes adopt the tucked in patterned shirts and immaculately pressed cream trousers look. House music blares from the speakers and drinks are downed at an alarming rate. It's all good fun.

Mon 12-5.30pm, Tue-Wed 12-11.30pm,
Thu-Sat 12pm – 2am, Sun 12-6pm
Meal for two: £22.90 (Pan fried Thai pork)

■ ■ Watershed Cafe/Bar/Cinema
1 Canon's Road, The Waterfront
(0117) 921 4135

With two cinemas, a gallery, digital gallery/cafe, conferencing rooms, darkrooms and a cafe/bar, there is enough for the artistically minded to be getting on with while the rest of us loaf. The café bar caters well for veggies and omnivores alike; I can't do the selection justice here so go and have a nose... although I must mention that they have Hoegaarden and Budvar on tap (a rare find). If you're into film, music, arts then this is the culture porthole in Bristol to be seen in, and thankfully it doesn't attract your usual glass-smashing idiot who thinks culture is something you find in a yoghurt pot.

Mon-Sat 11am-1pm, Sun 12am – 10.30pm
Meal for two: £20.15 (Meaty Main Option)

■ ■ Park Street Area

■ ■ Brasserie Pierre
44 Park Street (0117) 925 1139

Not exactly stylish bar culture here – think 80s vortex and you'll be close. However, it does serve up some admittedly classic bar meals for the suit trade at lunchtime. Dig into chicken supreme or charcoal grills for less than £7 and knock back a few beers while you're at it to help take your mind off the dodgy décor. The shameless thirtysomethings of Bristol pay mass homage to this place nightly and shake their booty to booming handbag until their corns hurt and they are forced to go home and act their age. Pitiful.

Mon-Sat 11.30am-2am, Sun 5pm-11.30pm
Meal for two: £ 21.40 (BBQ Burger)

■ ■ ■ Browns Restaurant & Bar
38 Queens Road, Clifton (0117) 930 4777
Big venue with more greenery than your local dope dealer. Mainly frequented by the young pro's (and a few old cons). Although part of a chain, it thankfully avoids the cheesy sameness of most bar-cum-restaurants. With both a bar and restaurant menu you'll be spoilt for choice. A classy joint with smiley staff and more nooks and crannies than you can shake a stick at.
Mon-Fri 11am-11.30pm,
Sat 10am-11.30pm, Sun 12-11pm
Meal for two: £26.85 (Traditional salmon cakes with lemon mayo and green salad)

■ ■ ■ The Elbow Room
64 Park Street (0117) 930 0242
Park Street has made room for the Elbow Room pool bar/restaurant so fling off your heels, forget your club wear and take a hike up to Park Street for a unique lounge experience. The designers behind the bar (which was first opened in 1995 in London) must be rubbing their hands with glee over the recent success and this bar is certainly successful. The stylised, sleek lines, booth seating and the purple pool tables downstairs attract the sophisticated pool sharks of Bristol, but you'll have to wait your turn as it

Sunday late licence
12.30am

E-shed

intelligent music every night from live dj's ranging from easy rolling vocal house to funk, hip hop & the latest in UK garage full daytime menu all under £6! tapas served until 1am Bristol's biggest Absinthe selection

Canon Road
Bristol
t: 0117 907 4287

gets very busy. The open fronted window looks onto the coolest street of Bristol and the view of the talent is worth popping in for alone.

Mon-Sat 12-2am, Sun 12-12.30am
Meal For Two: £27.15 (Chargrill Chicken)

■ ■ ■ Encore

10-11 Denmark Street (0117) 925 6678
Isit? is gone. Hurrah and bring on the Encore. A new bar sits in its place and Encore has turned the former musty wine bar into a respectable drinking hole. Pitched at the mature drinking market (is there such a thing?), and for those who fancy a tipple before they pop across the road into the Hippodrome for a show. No need to mind your Ps and Qs anymore, as this is a laid back kinda place. With traditional wooden furniture, racks of wine bottles and lanterns hanging above the bar, it's a warm intimate drinking experience away from the drink and puke policy of many bars. We like it.

Mon-Sat 12-11, Sun – closed
Meal For Two: £21.90 (Beef Rijorca)

■ ■ ■ Ether

2 Trenchard Street (0117) 922 6464
Big on style, small on space, but hey, that's the attraction with this place. There's no dress code, but if you're going to go scruffy then go with designer tat. Ether is seriously cool. With some of the best hip hop and funk sounds in the city as well as 60s style pod chairs, it attracts the crowds. The food ain't bad either, and although the drinks are um, not cheap, they do go to the trouble of pro-

jecting spinning psychedelic patterns onto the walls to save you from having to fork out for a tab of acid. Highly recommended.

■ ■ ■ Ha! Ha! Bar

20a Berkerley Square, Clifton
(0117) 927 7333

Blink and you'll miss this classy bar set off Park Street. Like most Ha Ha's they do the chain bar theme justice, which is truly refreshing. It hits the spot no matter what the occasion, casual drink or business lunch. Serving up soulful main courses aptly called 'proper food' as well as light 'nibble and munch' dishes if you're peckish. With oodles of outside seating, you're sure to find a spot to park your butt, whilst inside you have three rooms to choose from – you can loaf on a sofa, sit at a table or perch near the bar – so you know where we'll be then.

Mon-Fri 11am-11pm, Sat 10am-11pm,
Sun 10am-10.30pm.
Meal for two: £24.50 (Lime and coriander chicken salad)

■ ■ ■ **Le Chateau**
32 Park Street (0117) 926 8654
It's French. It's a café bar. It isn't a castle. Some one should tell them that this kind of thing is old hat now. Students who think they've got a bit of style are usually found in here. 'Nuff said.
Mon-Wed 9am-11pm, Thu-Sat 10-2am, Sun 12-11pm
Meal for Two: £24.95 (Grilled pork cutlet)

■ ■ ■ **The Park**
37 Triangle West, Clifton (0117) 940 6101
High ceilings, spacious interior and luxurious deep red couches. Very plush. Very stylish. Very comfortable. This place is home to the beautiful people, but if you're looking for a bottled blonde, you can purchase one over the bar. That would be Leffe Blonde, the Belgian beer. What did you think I meant? The food's pretty damn good too and as far as the music goes, there's everything from jazz to hip hop. Have we nothing bad to say about the place? Actually, no, we haven't. Something for everyone. Pure class.
Mon-Thu 11am-11pm, Fri & Sat 11am-1am

■ ■ **Whiteladies Road**

■ ■ **Bar Humbug**
89 Whiteladies Rd (0117) 904 0061
Frequented by Whiteladies' café society by day and a younger, funkier crowd by night, Humbug is always packed. And with good reason. It's the perfect pre-club venue. Bright yellow walls, asymmetric iron artwork, DJs and a decent choice of drinks including some rather lethal (and strangely named) cocktails. You know you're pissed when you find yourself ordering a 'I'm Very

HA! HA! Bar & Canteen

YOUR GUIDE TO munching crunching dribbling bubbling slurping guzzling

bringing the HA! HA! experience...

tel: 0117 927 7333
20a Berkeley Square, Clifton, Bristol
www.hahaonline.co.uk

enjoy!

Naughty And I Promise Not To Do It Again While You're Looking'. One of the trendiest bars in the UK – so we're told. Hard to speak for the nation, but it certainly holds true for Bristol.
Mon-Thu 5pm-11pm, Fri & Sat 1pm-11pm, Sun 12pm-10.30pm.
Meal for two: £23.75 (Steak & salad)

■ ■ ■ The Fine Line
59 Whiteladies Road (0117) 973 7727
Taking centre stage on Whiteladies this trendy wine bar likes to think it's somewhat classy in all respects. Bringing the West End combo of bland, contemporary Brit style and chic French windows to Bristol. Split into two parts, one serves up a mix of Australasian/Med food in the formal restau-

rant, and the other is strictly for drinking. Be warned though, don't cross the 'fine line' or you'll be quickly asked to move, no matter how elaborate the excuse (believe me I've tried). You'll find it about three miles up its own arse, but if you like that air of arrogance you'll fit in here.
Mon-Sat 11am-11pm
Meal for two: £25.70 (Smoked Salmon)

■ ■ Henry J Beans
95 Whiteladies Rd (0117) 974 3794
US theme bars – you either love 'em or hate 'em. If you can stick the 'authentic' décor then get down there for cheap as chips cocktails, shooters and spirits (selected drinks reduced by a further £1 between 5 and 7 on weekdays). The menu is a fairly uninspiring Tex-Mex affair, but it's cheap and fills a hole – much like most of the blokes on the pull in here. The clientele consists of piss-poor students, forty-something tightwads and guys called Brad.
Mon-Sat 12-11pm, Sun 12-10.30
Meal for two: £20.90 (Deluxe Express sandwich)

■ ■ Henry Africa's Hothouse
65, Whiteladies Road (0117) 923 8300
Full of your happy-go-lucky shop assistants and loaded students. The Hothouse sits at the start of the Whiteladies strip with challenging revolving doors, presumably to keep the idiots out – it hasn't worked.
Mon-Fri 4-11pm, Sat 10-11pm, Sun 12-10.30pm
Meal For Two: £29.85 (Fajitas)

pubs

www.itchybristol.co.uk

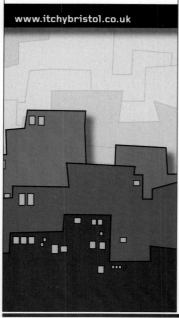

Opening times are 11/12ish-11.30 Mon-Sat, 12-10.30 Sun unless otherwise stated.

■ ■ ■ Whiteladies Road

Nicknamed 'The Strip' due to the many watering holes and restaurants. So starting from the top, here we go...

■ ■ ■ The Blackboy Inn
171 Whiteladies Road (0117) 940 6130
Cosy little pub near the top of Whiteladies Road. Apparently it's been there since 1787 and judging by the décor it's not had a revamp since it was built. It's split into two rooms, both with carpets that your nan'd kill for. The front room fills up with lovely lasses with tractor accents and the back bar is home to the sports fanatics who gaze at the shrine to Bristol Rugby Club in the corner. They don't appear to be shy in here; check out the picture of the boys in blue in the buff. With a cracking jukebox and live sports you get the feeling they'd do anything to drag you in here. And that's not a bad thing. Warm, friendly and fully clothed (most of the time).
Food Served: 12-3pm Mon-Sat

■ ■ ■ The Bohemia
168 Whiteladies Road (0117) 973 9522
If all makeovers were as good as this, we'd all be supermodels. A popular pub at the top of Whiteladies Strip with numerous levels culminating with a roof garden. Brushed red walls, rustic wrought iron, chandeliers and bold colours make the place feel like a stately home. A pre club or start to a night out of raucous partying. Two big screens show all of the live sporting events while on the third floor you'll find two pool tables. Serves up an

adventurous cocktail and shooters list along with local beers and spirits such as Smiles and Courage. Notoriously busy on weekends when the queues start forming and the noise levels get turned up. Definitely one to put on your list.

Food Served: 12-3pm, 7pm-10pm Mon-Fri, 12-4 Sat & Sun

■ ■ Dog & Duck

44 Whiteladies Rd (0117) 973 8857

Next to the ABC that's battling to save its life, and by the looks of things it could be contagious. They've saved on wallpaper by sticking posters of every movie to have played next door on the walls and ceilings. Split into two levels with the lower pool room seedily lit with coloured wall lights and Jack Daniel's candlelit bottles. Upstairs you can get sozzled on cheap cocktails such as the infamous Plastic Gangster for £2.95 or the usual Bull concoction for £3.75. With the drinks this cheap and food from £1.50 it's unsurprisingly littered with impoverished students.

■ ■ Rat and Parrot

71-73 Whiteladies Road (0117) 973 0534

Bloody huge, deceptively stretching far back from the road. The outside seating areas aren't the wisest choice unless you enjoy the sweet smell of exhaust smoke, so you're better off grabbing one of the few thousand seats inside. As in most cities, The Rat is heaving come the weekend, although the average IQ levels only just stretch into double figures. There's a quick nod towards Michelangelo with the mural that stretches along the back wall, but don't try and start a discussion about the great man – most people in here think he serves pizza at Renato's down the road. Fun and games come in the form of giant Jenga and Connect Four, but there's better games to play – like spot the potential underage drinker.

Food Served: 11-6 Mon-Sun

■ ■ Park Street Area

■ ■ The Berkeley

15-19 Queen's Road (0117) 927 9550

Another cog in the massive chain that is Wetherspoons. The Berkeley plays host to an unfussy crowd from crusty old duffers to loud student rugby teams. The trademark lack of music and soiled carpets are present here. Cheap, in all senses, with two meals for £5.50 and a mixed grill for meat lovers for £5.49. No real sense of atmosphere, just lairy, pissed lads and lasses who down the deals. Aftershock is £1.50 a shot, Smirnoff Ice, WKD just £1.79 and Reef at an obscene £1.09. Cask ales make guest appearances with Directors and Theakstons on regular tap and the usual Stella at £1.35 a pint. Clearly the prices are the best thing about this place.

Food Served: 12-10pm Mon-Thu, Fri & Sat 12-8pm, Sun 12-9

A MELLOW MIX OF SPIRIT AND SOUL. THAT FLAVOURS WHATEVER IT TOUCHES.

■ ■ ■ Bunch Of Grapes
Denmark Street (0117) 955 0601

Top on the itchy 'must go and have a pint' list, and all that a proper pub should be. Appealing hugely to the theatrical and thespian luvvies who order their pre-show drinks before nipping across the road to watch performances at the Hippodrome. Dark wood interior with padded wall seats and scattered stools. Intimate and cosy even with the red ceiling. Theatrical posters line the walls from the year dot to Jesus Christ Superstar. The bar is full of obscure cask ales such as Sunny Daze and Uley bitter alongside all your usual suspects. It's renowned for its live music with the Bristol blues line-up on Friday night and Just Jazz on Saturday. Sunday takes a more humorous approach with live local comedy. A brilliant start or finish to any night. Highly recommended. Weekly entertainment and listings can be found at itchybristol.co.uk.

■ ■ ■ The Greenhouse
37 College Green (0117) 927 6426

Greeny-blue outside with an explosion of tin, tiles and glass bits stuck in the walls inside. Despite the artistic undertones it will take a lot more than a neon lit face with a screen ejecting from its gob to convince anyone with more than half a brain cell to drink here. Apparently, the place was designed to be illuminated from all angles, but the orange and purple ceiling is loud enough to be seen from a distant planet. 'Shabby' and 'hole' are two words that spring to mind in this multi-levelled pub-cum-bar.

Famous for their cocktails and partying, but most sane people will see this as hell on earth.
Food Served: 12-9.30pm Mon-Wed, 12-7pm Thu, 12-6pm Fri-Sun

■ ■ ■ The Hatchett
Frogmore Street (0117) 929 4118

The Hatchett can't decide when they were established, so we'll take an educated guess of circa 15th century – but don't quote me. One of Bristol's landmark pubs ideally placed by The Rock, Ether and the newly opened Sushi restaurant so you're spoilt for choice, but you should take time out to look in here. Hugely popular with pre-clubbers and students who congregate outside on the patio areas to drink at weekends. There's a whole host of deals and events starting on Tuesday with a meal deal and pint for £4.50. From Thursday to Saturday the place rocks 'til 1am with bottle promos, karaoke and DJs.
Food Served: Mon-Fri 12-2am, Sat 12-3pm, Sun 12-2.30pm

■ ■ ■ The White Hart
54-58 Park Row (0117) 945 6060

Situated amidst the ultra-hip skate and surf shops of Park Row and a member of the 'It's A Scream' group. It escapes chain-pub blandness by boasting colourful walls and Aboriginal shindigs everywhere. The notable Scream mask is used as wall lights to help you weave your way through numerous rooms. Dishing up food and drink deals to the student brigade and hooded skate crews who pile in to watch the MTV screens, play on the pink pool tables and raid the gum ball machines – it's more of an amusement arcade than a boozer. A bright, simple place ideal for watching the footy or meeting your mates.
Food Served: Mon-Sat 12-7pm, Sun 1-7

■ ■ ■ Town Centre/Waterfront

■ ■ ■ The Brasshouse
**Cannons Rd, The Waterfront
(0117) 922 0330**

Part of the drag of bars along the Waterfront, this huge pub is a convenient pit stop with tourists, suits and townies alike. Yes, it's full of brass (I feel pitifully sorry for the cleaners), but you shouldn't be here to admire the ornaments. Next to the ever-popular Evolution club, and competing with the banging sounds next door on Friday when the DJs move in. The overspill of casualties litter the outside seating area to escape the pounding tracks. Saturday and Sunday are less alarming with funky soul being the dish of the day. It's actually more popular for its food than entertainment. We recommend their hot baguettes, such as the Steak and Dijon mustard for £4.95, and wash it down with a cheap bottle of house wine for a fiver.
Food Served: 12-11 Mon-Sun

■ ■ ■ The Commercial Rooms
42-43 Corn St (0117) 927 9681

Well, you should be familiar with the Wetherspoons trademark features by now, and this place ain't much different. Huge palatial pub with putrid orange, red and cream walls; this JD has gone for the more 'distinguished' look with huge original oil paintings of Brunel, and some old trout, whose name escapes me. We're talking seriously big, but size doesn't equate to atmosphere. The noise exceeds several decibels at the weekend and the flesh wall of shirted twats makes the bar impossible to reach. Cheap food – as you expect, and big loos. So if you're financially challenged, colour blind and incontinent, you'll love it.
*Food Served: 10.30-10 Mon-Sat,
10.30-9.30 Sun*

■ ■ ■ The Famous Old Duke
King Street (0117) 927 7137

The atmosphere in here is electric. Even if you're not a fan of live non-stop jazz music, you'll undoubtedly be swept up by the enthusiasm of everybody else. Its excellent reputation is well-earned and it pulls in both a live act and a good crowd every night of the week. With a real unique vibe and Courage, Smiles and Directors behind the bar, the place is popular – and rightly so. One of Bristol's finest entertainment venues and watering holes.
Food Served: 11-6 Mon-Sat

■ ■ ■ The Llandoger Trow
King Street (0117) 926 0783
Gorgeous pub near the water. A huge Tudor style front spills over onto the street echoing the naval docking days of Bristol. The cobbles outside are precarious for high heeled ladeez but provide the odd moment of hilarity when some lose their footing. Inside, the flag stone floors, master fireplaces and alcoves just make you want to move in. Split into two enchanting levels where you can captain your crew over dinner or be a happy sailor at the bar. Eat, drink and be merry, it's Olde England at its best.
Food: 12–7pm

■ ■ ■ O'Neill's
18-24 Baldwin Street (0117) 945 8891
OK, it serves Guinness. And there's a sign above the door boasting 'Good Craic', not forgetting the token Celtic 'failte' loo signs. But let's be fair, this pub has an atmosphere that's about as authentically Irish as a plate

of pasta. It's more reminiscent of a scary ski-resort than an Irish boozer, especially in the downstairs dancefloor (you know – packed out, chart pop blasting, multicoloured disco lights, middle-aged men dancing). But hey, there's still plenty of good drinks promotions to help get you as drunk as a (Irish) skunk, and indulge in, erm, shenanigans.
12-11pm Mon–Wed, 12-1am Thu,
12-2am Fri & Sat, 12-10.30pm Sun
Food served all day 'til close.

top 5 for...
Playing Pool
1. Elbow Room (Bar)
2. The Bohemia
3. Dog & Duck
4. White Hart
5. Finnegan's Wake

■ ■ ■ Old Fish Market
59-63 Baldwin Street (0117) 921 1515
Perhaps not the most inviting name for a pub, but don't let that put you off. Traditional ale and pie pub with more mural paintings than the Louvre. Massive in size with lots of table and barrel/carousel style seating so you can rest those pegs. Stocking a great range of cask ales including Chiswick, Smiles and London Pride with a separate dining area that dishes up some tasty pub grub. Numerous picture frames glorify the pub's obsession with its history, so admire the old fish market

PLAN YOUR RESIGNATION TACTICALLY

s you tuck into your cod. Ideal for a pub lunch or to watch the sport on the big screen TV. A reliable port of call anytime of the day.
Food Served: 12– 9pm Mon-Thu,
12-8pm Fri-Sun

■ ■ The Toad

1 Corn Street (0117) 945 9990

More of a stately home than a pub. The Toad comes complete with pillars, leather sofas, high ceilings and more plants than Kew Gardens but don't let that put you off. The pub is split into seating and standing areas with a dancefloor at the far end of the building. It's the preferred business lunch venue of the nearby office staff, and a regular port of call for the pre-clubbing crowd. You can watch the sport on any one of the numerous TVs, but you'd do well to make it down for 'Wicked' Thursdays when selected bottles and pints are £1.50. No toads though.
Food Serving Times: 12-7pm Mon-Sat
Mon-Wed 11-11pm, Thu-Sat 12-2am

■ ■ Walkabout

0 Corn Street (0117) 930 0181

At the top end of Corn Street lies The Walkabout. It's essential that if you enter here you abandon all hope of enjoying yourself... unless, of course, you're a student, a divorcee or an arsehole. A constant stream of bad music, bad live acts and 2-4-1 on offers on badly poured pints and bottles. The place is scarily big, and even more scarily, it's usually rammed – it wouldn't be so bad if it was rammed full of Aussies so we could keep them all in one place, but the people of Bristol appear to love it. Hopefully, they'll all grow up and realise that this is no way to spend a night out. The 'fun' continues upstairs in the Surfers Paradise club which is open 'til 1am Thur-Sat. One redeeming factor is that they show almost every sporting event going – which is great – if you don't mind watching as Mambo No.5 booms out over the commentary.
Food Serving Times: 12-11pm Mon-Sat,
12-9.30pm Sun

■ ■ Clifton

Clifton and Clifton Village have got so many watering holes we've had to minimise it down to a sprinkling of good, bad and average. A part of town made for an all day bender, so if you're up for it check out the following...

REMEMBER, LEAVE ON A POSITIVE NOTE.

■ ■ ■ The Clifton
16 Regent Street (0117) 974 6321

Average boozer in the heart of Clifton Village. Made famous in these parts for the karaoke, and if previous visits are anything to go by it's worth bringing some ear plugs. Out of the cracks come medallion-swinging locals who fiercely compete with the students to win the much 'coveted' first prize on Thursday nights. So make an arse out of yourself – everyone else does. The opening bars of 'Dancing Queen', and 'I Will Survive' usually turn my stomach, but if it's your thing, you'll love it.

Mon-Thurs 11am-3pm, 5pm-11pm,
Fri & Sat 11-11pm, Sun 12-10.30pm
No Food Served

■ ■ ■ The Clifton Wine Bar
4 Richmond Terrace, Clifton
(0117) 973 2069

Home to all the students in Clifton during term time who return the following morning to recover with an all day brekkie. Cavernous is one way to describe this place, but popular would be most fitting. The stone basement is enhanced by several little nooks and crannies that are filled with sofas and coffee tables, but the flagstone floor and vine garden win hands down as the place to settle down. The jugs are the most popular order of the night (the drink kind that is) and at £7.50, they're good value too. A massive wine list is chalked up for all to see, and mainline brews and spirits adorn the bar (6X at £1.90 and Stella at £2 a pint

are particular favourites). You can wine, dine or recline in one of the rooms on a hard back chair or squidgy sofa. Not that you'll care where you're sitting after you've had a skinful anyway.

Food Served: 11-11pm Mon-Sat,
11-10.30pm Sun

■ ■ ■ The Hophouse
16 Kings Road (0117) 923 7390

Bang in tune with its locals and students alike with a recent internet access point added in the Surf Shack. On the lower level a clock dangles precariously over the student crowd who arrive en masse to make the most of the 20% discounts on offer (to get one you have to buy a quid key ring and produce an NUS card). Upstairs is like stepping into a café bar on Whiteladies strip; it's decked out with cane furniture laced with cream and coral walls and attracts a more mature crowd. Well worth tucking into some food, especially from the specials board

which is great value. Bring the parents and you can leave them sipping a coffee while you join your mates downstairs.
Internet access £1 for 20 mins.
12-3pm, 7pm-10pm Mon-Fri, 12-3, 11-10pm Sat, 12-3, 7-9.30 Sun

■ ■ ■ The Lansdown
8 Clifton Road (0117) 973 4949

The Lansdown is next to the smart Muset restaurant with its modern art and toffee nosed clientele, so walk on by and have a pint in here. A warm, cosy pub that does the best cocktails in town (well, Clifton anyway). There's even a beer garden where they hold decent BBQs in the summer, and a cracking sundeck at the back of the garden if you're after some privacy. Happy hour runs from 4 'til 7 so get there early and get plastered for a couple of quid. Bring it on.
Food Served: 4-9.30 Mon-Fri, 4-9 Sat & Sun, Sunday lunch from 12pm

■ ■ ■ Gloucester Road

■ ■ ■ The Bristol Comedy Pub
117-119 Stokes Croft (0117) 903 0796
It looks like a fruit bowl inside with all that green and orange on the walls, but at least you can take your pick of the entertainment on offer. There are two rooms, each offering a different flavour. The back room has live music, comedy and theatre performances, and a ticket will set you back a couple of quid. The bar is located in the front room amidst the bright surroundings. DJs play nightly: Tuesday is reggae night whilst Wednesday is home for funk lovers, Thursday plays drum 'n' bass and Friday covers car wash disco tunes. The last night of the week hosts electronica and laid back jazz. Something for almost everyone. Guaranteed a decent night whenever you visit.
Tue-Sat 5pm-1am, Mon 5pm-11pm, closed Sun
Food Served: 5pm-12.30am Tue-Sat

■ ■ ■ The Hobgoblin
69-71 Gloucester Road (0117) 940 1611
Very lively pub with more plants and hanging baskets than a garden centre. Traditional all the way, stocking a vast number of local and obscure beers on tap. Entertainment comes in the form of sports that are shown daily. Raucous chanting and hissing is mandatory behaviour in here. Not exactly a quiet place at night, probably something to do with a discount card that entitles you to cheap booze if you're a pesky student, but

THE WORLD'S BEST CITY

you gotta flex your NUS or they won't give you one, and photocopies won't do either – believe me I've tried.
No Food Served

■ ■ ■ St Michaels Hill & Cotham

■ ■ ■ Finnegan's Wake
31-35 Cotham Hill (0117) 973 3793

No prizes for guessing that this is an Irish boozer. So expect the gaudy green exterior, pub fare and ripped off slogans slapped about. What was it that Oscar Wilde said – 'Moderation is a fatal thing, nothing succeeds like excess', and oh yes, the students and locals certainly do that here. Six pumps of Guinness and Irish Harp keep the punters happy, and they make sure that they keep up that great Irish tradition of getting slaughtered at every available opportunity. Sky Sports is on throughout the day, so you can keep up to date with the latest ten pin bowling championships. Upstairs, you'll find two pool tables but you'll need a cue unless you want to look really stupid, so ask behind the bar, and for £2 they'll give you one.
Food Served: 11-9.30 Mon-Sat,
12-9.30 Sun

■ ■ ■ The Highbury Vaults
St Michaels Hill (0117) 973 3203

There's been a pub here since the 1850s. Before that it was used for less pleasurable activities, such as housing the local villains in the vaults. Nowadays, this much loved Youngs pub houses students and locals who are here of their own accord. Olde style artefacts adorn the walls of a boozer that is renowned for two things – its good beer and the back garden. A network of pokey rooms and corridors lead to what I've overheard described as paradise, but that's a tad strong, so lets just say it's impressive. A subtle red wooden bench, gas heaters to provide a warm glow, and a canopy of vines draped over a wooden pergoda – it's not your average beer garden. A classic pub that serves decent food at pub prices.
Food Served: Mon-Fri 12-3pm,
5.30pm-9pm, Sat & Sun 12-3pm

■ ■ ■ The White Bear
16 Kings Road (0117) 929 7265

Can be seen from a distance due to the 6ft white polar bear sitting above the door. Not a common sight in Bristol. Brimming with old style artefacts and deceased butterflies in a hammock placed above the bar with a red leg hanging out – presumably one of those inebriated students who never made the Uni library. Drinks are cheap and draught pints are reduced all day Mon-Thu and 'til 7pm Fri-Sun. It's the ideal training ground for all discerning students who need to brush up on that hand-to-mouth technique.
Food Served: 12-7 Mon-Sun

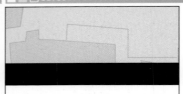

cafés

www.itchybristol.co.uk

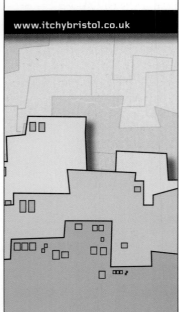

■ ■ A La Bonne Bouche
120 St Michael's Hill
(0117) 929 8113
Crowded at lunchtime, but well worth the wait. Nourishing, carefully prepared food, reasonably priced and close to the University (but only infrequently cluttered with students). Friendly, yet sophisticated.
Soup of the day and baguette,
£1.30 to take away, £1.80 to eat in

■ ■ Black and White Café
27 Grosvenor Rd, St. Paul's
(0117) 942 0437
This place is still massively popular, and with good reason. Serving the best West Indian food in the whole of Bristol, they've got a separate seating area dedicated to the privilege, and a pool table at just 50p.
Open 7 days a week 10.30am-1am

■ ■ Blue Juice
39 Cotham Hill (0117) 973 4800
A wet-dream for health food freaks; everything is made from fruit or vegetables. Take a seat at the breakfast bar or sit outside and watch the toxin-ridden world go by.
Freshly squeezed orange juice £1.80,
tuna wrap £2.40

■ ■ Boston Tea Party
75 Park Street (0117) 929 8601
The best-known coffee shop in Bristol, and the busiest. Two floors furnished with sofas, coffee tables and half a dozen pleasantly garish paintings, plus a smashing garden outside, complete with canopies and heaters. The food's healthy and delicious, and served to you by friendly, efficient staff.
Cappuccino £1.40 Soup £2.75

■ ■ The Bristolian Café
Picton St, Montpelier (07866) 891196

Weekends are extremely busy with locals prepared to queue out the door for their famous pancakes (served Sat & Sun only). One of the few true remaining independent cafés in Bristol. Brightly coloured inside and out, all art on the walls is for sale and one of the artists likes it there so much that he even works there. We love it muchly.
Mon-Sat 9-4. Sun 9.30-3.30. Closed Wed.
American style pancakes with fresh fruit salad, yoghurt and maple syrup £3.75

■ ■ Ch'A
82 Park Street (0117) 929 1097
A bewildering variety of tea and snacks make Ch'A worth a visit. Only a few doors down from Starbucks, but a far better choice.
Tea £1.20, sandwiches £1.95

■ ■ Coffee One
Under construction as we went to print but expect an individual coffee experience from this new chain of coffee bars in the South West. Chic environment with neutral tone décor, slouch sofas and 'proper' coffee served up by friendly staff. Other branches include Cardiff and Bath.

top 5 for...
Breakfast Fry-Ups

1. York Café
2. Elysee Snack Bar
3. St Michael's Café
4. Café 2000
5. Edwards

■■ Goodbean Coffee
Blackwell's, 89 Park St (0117) 925 6055

Coffee and books in one shop. It doesn't get much better than this. A superb concept that has been sadly overlooked – until now.
Cappuccino £1.90

■■ Millers
55 Queens Road (0117) 914 6549

They never ever ask you to leave here, even if the most you have bought is a coffee you finished an hour ago – and with a garden, fantastic toilets and sofas downstairs, this is the ideal spot to doss out. Open 'til 10pm on Wednesdays, Thursdays and Fridays.
Cappuccino £1.60, soup of the day £3.20

■■ Starbucks
78 Park Street (0117) 922 0863

No-smoking policy. Don't encourage them.
Caramel macchiata and biscotti, £2.95

■■ York Café
1 York Place (0117) 923 9656

The speciality is the aptly named Monster breakfast, but if you want to be kind to your arteries you can still get a decent meal any time of day.
Coffee 60p, Monster fried breakfast £3.95

■■ Internet Cafés

■■ Bristol Life.co.uk
Baldwin Street

Get that caffeine hit before arriving, a there's no coffee here. Instead, it's down to business with one of the 40 PCs. Bit like being back in the office really, but without the boss giving you a bollocking for accessing www.hothornycheerleaders.com. Web training is on offer for internet virgins.

■■ Easycaf.com
108a Stokes Croft (0117) 924 1999

Well off the beaten track so you'll have to search this one out, but it's worth it for the first rate service and advice. Check out www.itchybristol.co.uk and relax with a coffee in front of the screen.

■■ Internet Exchange
23-25 Queens Road, Clifton (0117) 929 8026

Particularly busy during lunchtime when half of Bristol's office crowd pour in to e-mail in peace. They offer e-mail, internet access, scanning, printing, faxing, PC games and online learning.
Free membership, internet access and email from 3p per minute

■■ OnCoffee.net
11 Christmas Steps (0117) 925 1100

Serves up the best coffee around as well as some great food, making it a good stop for even the most technologically challenged amongst you. Intimate, friendly and the best place in Bristol to log on. And you should know by now where to point your browser.

gay

www.itchybristol.co.uk

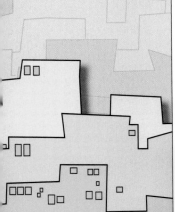

■■■ Club Castro
72-73 Old Market Street (07899) 881 073
This club insists on an attitude free zone. They no longer hold fetish nights and have just completed a major refurbishment. They promote a gay mixed, friendly and caring policy and this is strictly enforced – no tantrums here. They do this by expecting you to become a member which costs £10. However, you're allowed in three times before you get hassled – their computer monitors punters' attendance. With an underground hard house vibe plus a sprinkling of trance, this club packs 'em in, filling all three floors most Saturdays.
Wed closed/Thurs 8-2am/Fri 10-6am/1st & 3rd Sat 10-8am/2nd & 4th Sat 10-6am/Sun 10-4am. Fri-Sun after-club 'til midday.

■■ The Elephant
20 St Nicholas Street (0117) 925 2820
Decorated in the traditional pub style complete with sofas, loud music and cheerful staff. All ages and sexualities are welcome and with a cabaret on Sundays, there's usually a substantial transvestite crowd. There's strippers on the last Friday of the month, karaoke on Wednesdays and bingo on Tuesdays run by two luscious drag queens.
Food served 12-3

in association with gay.uk.net

The Griffin
41 Colston St. (0117) 927 2421

A small triangular pub, the Griffin is curious but friendly. It's decorated in orange and green and adorned with homoerotic artwork, which can play havoc with your head after one too many. The regulars are very friendly, sometimes to the point of being overwhelming if you're not used to it. At weekends you'll find Bristol's first Dutch style cruise bar with occasional theme nights for those with particular tastes, all housed upstairs. Not for the faint hearted.

The Old Castle Green
4b Gloucester Lane, Old Market
(0117) 955 0925

You should spot this place by the huge rainbow flag outside. Pleasant and friendly, renowned for its chilled and somewhat romantic atmosphere (candlelit tables), this is a great place to have a relaxing pint. A mixed gay crowd attends, Friday nights being the busiest. There's a disco once every five weeks on a Saturday and a beer garden for those lovely summer evenings.
Mon-Thurs 12-2.30pm, 5-11pm
Fri 12-11pm/Sat-Sun 7-11pm

The Pineapple
37 St. George St. (0117) 907 1162

The Pineapple has recently been refurbished and the end result is a dramatic improvement to the interior of the pub, with a brighter and far more welcoming atmosphere. It's the ideal place to have a few quiet drinks or play a game or two of pool. With a friendly and young clientele, it's also a good place to meet your homo pals before moving to one of the nearby clubs.

The Queenshilling
9 Frogmore Street (0117) 926 4342

This is the place to see and be seen. Refurbished last year, The Queenshilling is friendly and welcoming to all ages, genders and sexualities. It doesn't open very late, but the place is usually heaving by 10pm, especially on weekends. Playing mainly commercial dance music, the club also regularly puts on live bands, but doesn't do karaoke anymore. R'n'B lovers should come along on Tuesdays, whilst students have a dedicated night on Thursday.
Mon-Thurs 9-2am/Fri-Sat 9-3am
Sun 9-1am with a 12.30am licence

Winns
23-25 West Street, Old Market
(0117) 941 4024

A fairly new place, opened on the site of an old bank. There's a large main room and dancefloor, as well as a pool room and internet computer. If you want a quieter place to have a drink and a chat there's a second smaller bar away from the dancefloor. Students get discounts on entry and are treated very well by the friendly staff.
Regular pub hours

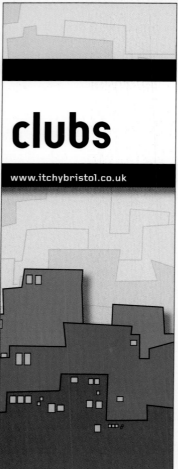

clubs

www.itchybristol.co.uk

■ ■ ■ Bierkeller

The Pithay, All Saints St (0117) 926 8514

The Keller made its name as one of the best rock venues in Bristol, but it's working to shake off that reputation and has reinvented itself as one of the best alternative venues in the city. It's the kinda place that you're likely to catch good bands on the way up, and with a totally obscure music policy, it's attracting a weird and wonderful clientele. Punk, indie, rock... you name it, they'll host a night dedicated to it. 'Cocksoc' – oh, the puns escape me – is a night dedicated to cocktails with a litre's worth at just £6.50. The strange music policy is taken a step too far on Saturdays with a live Oompah band. Shouldn't work – but it does. Slip on the lederhosen and get lagered up with the rest of Bristol.

■ ■ ■ Blue Mountain Club

Stokescroft (0117) 924 6666

The Mountain is one of those clubs that doesn't try to be cool, it just is. There's a decent sized dancefloor, as well as a slightly quieter upstairs area and balcony. Playing the best funk, breaks & beats, hip hop and house in a suitably dark, on-the-edge environment, it's popular with practically everyone – apart from the tracksuit clad Hanhamites, that is.

■ ■ ■ Café Blue

Old Fire Station, Silver St (0117) 904 3329

The Café Blue club sits proudly in the former old fire station in the town centre. Reputably known for dishing out the best in live music and entertainment. With three levels to hike up, five bars and a VIP room it's consistently presented the best of the best to the hungry clubbing masses. It's not your average club

Finger tips

RIZLA **It's what you make of it.**

www.rizla.com

with nice carpets, bright walls and a jazzy décor. This autumn will see the established drum 'n' bass student night 'Locus' and an incredible line up of artists take over the joint on Tuesdays. The regular indie night is on Wednesdays, and 'Blue print' on Thursdays has seen the likes of Artful Dodger, the Dreem Team and DJ Luck & MC Neat at Café Blue. The popular drum 'n' bass outfit 'Mutiny', take up a residency slot on Fridays with big name DJs at other times. Saturday sessions see 'Out of the Blue' and a frenzy of house lovers partying 'til 4am. Previous acts that have performed here include Fragma, Timo Maas, The Freestylers, Jeremy Healey, Jon Pleased Wimmin, Norman Jay, Scratch Perverts and Side Stepper. Plenty going on then.

■ ■ ■ Club Crème
46 West Street, St Phillips (07967) 251 398
Half a dozen gorgeous naked babes (and one ugly one) shaking the best bristols in Bristol in your face. And I was forced to review this. Have I got the best job in the world or have I got the best job in the world?

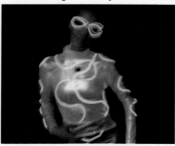

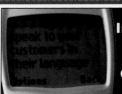

■ ■ ■ The Cooler
48 Park Street (0117) 945 0999
The Cooler has become the student landmark in Park Street and has steadfastly served them well. Inside it's like an explosion in a paint factory with garish yellow, blue and red walls. It's part of the 'It's a Scream' chain but shuns the usual scream ethos despite the décor. The club has two bars, table seating and a dancefloor and is hopefully soon to be refurbished. The music policy has seen a sharp turn around in recent years and is now a pick 'n' mix affair of indie and rock on Mondays, cheesy tunes on Tuesdays and salsa and Latino on Wednesdays. Thursdays is the real heavyweight with the all new 'Technique' where

Hot tip

you'll come across the finest in drum 'n' bass, electronica, beats & breaks and a sprinkling of hip hop courtesy of the likes of Deck Wrecka and Ed Rush. The 'Fridaze' sessions at The Cooler see classic funk, soul, hip hop and Motown belt from the decks before Saturdays 'Ascension' with the best of soul, ragga, swing and hip hop from Ed Kase, the Killer Tonic Crew and Ladies Touch. Cooler than your average club then.

■ ■ Cosies
Portland Square (0117) 942 4110
More of a late bar than a club, it's a seriously chilled venue in a cavern; a totally cheese-free zone. A very cosy venue (for cosy, read cramped and sweaty) showcasing the best of local talent. DJs spinning dub, reggae, hip hop, drum 'n' bass. So for a taste of the real Bristol, this can't be beaten. Better still, entrance is indecently cheap.

■ ■ Creation
13-21 Baldwin Street (0117) 922 7177
Since its inception in November '99, Creation has built itself an unparalleled reputation throughout the South West for staging some of the most credible club events in the UK. With national names such as Slinky, The Boutique, Progression Sessions and Full Cycle making the place their second home and world-renowned DJs Tim Westwood and Trevor Nelson selecting Creation for their only residencies out of London, Creation's promotional stable offers underground sounds and cutting edge live shows, right across the broad spectrum of dance. You can choose from two dancefloors, four bars and the best sound, lighting and visual environments technology has to offer. This club blends the stainless steel minimalism of the main auditorium with the plush decadence of the more intimate lounge room bar. As the generous viewing balconies overlook the central auditorium, so the glass walled lounge room looks out across the sunken dancefloor. A sublime mixture of simplicity, style and comfort, Creation is worth a look any night of the week.

■ ■ Dojo Lounge
Park Row (0117) 925 1177
Blink and you'd miss it. And that'd be a real shame as this is one of the best clubs in Bristol. It's small – but size isn't everything,

driven
by music

FEATURING:

soul
slinky
galaxy
drive by
westwood
safe house

bubblegum
experience
the boutique
logical progression

driven
by music

CREATION . 13-21 BALDWIN STREET . BRISTOL . BS1 1NA . INFO: 0117 945 0959
creation@ukdanceclubs.co.uk . www.ukdanceclubs.co.uk

ight girls? – but perfectly formed. It's popular – so expect to queue for entrance as well as drinks, but the wait is worthwhile – a cracking venue bringing the best in hip hop and progressive beats. Despite the crowds, the Dojo retains an exclusive (if slightly sweaty) atmosphere. But even the sweat factor has been considered, and the roof terrace opens to let in some much needed air at the weekend. Definitely one for those who are serious about their music. Best avoided by fake-tanned slappers looking for a leg-over.

■ ■ The Depot
7 Lawrence Hill (0117) 954 1608
This relative newcomer to the Bristol scene is really starting to make an impact. Situated in what used to be the bus drivers' social club, it has thankfully reinvented itself since those heady days. In fact, the only sign that this used to be a meeting place for weary transport workers is the name. Acting as a snooker club during the day and music venue at night, The Depot caters for the hardcore techno-heads of Bristol. It's a bitch to get to, but worth the taxi fare if you're into techno gabba, progressive mixes and rough and tuff disco. There's a decent enough bar, and if you get there early you can still shoot a few rounds of pool.

■ ■ Evolution
**The Harbourside, Canons Road
(0117) 922 0330**
Identikit punters in townie paradise. Great fun to be had with the huge queues in the winter for window-clubbers. What's a win-

dow-clubber, I hear you ask? Well, that'd be the sort of sick individual who dresses up in suitably warm clobber, carefully dons balaclava and leather gloves and throws snowballs at the poor freezing tartlets who have clearly misjudged the season and are wearing little more than bikinis. Manage to dodge the snowballs long enough and you'll find yourself in a popular mainstream club with two rooms, one dedicated to club anthems, the other playing Brit Pop. Hell on earth. But if you really must relive those Ibiza days, then at least visit on a Tuesday – it's student night so the entrance and drinks are cheap. Chances of a shag? High. Just remember to take the wedding ring off.

■ ■ The Fez Club
26-28 St Nicholas Street (0117) 925 9200
Moroccan themed club. Another one. It's the same as all the other Moroccan theme clubs all over the country. As Moroccan themed clubs go, this is one of the best – with red velvet booth seating and quiet areas where you can hear yourself think. Live sets, a decent selection of dance, R'n'B, house, garage and trance throughout the week. And not a camel in sight.

RIZLA + www.rizla.com

■ ■ ■ Lakota
Stokescroft (0117) 942 6208

Lakota is one of the better-known clubs in Bristol, mainly because they employ those annoyingly gorgeous teenagers to press flyers into your hand. Once a top club, the crown has slipped and we at itchy were determined to find out why. The answer to this came in the form of Hans, a German tourist, who spotting us armed with pen, pad and camera, sidled over. 'Iz ve bezt techo gabba,' he said. We smiled politely. 'You muzt write eet down. Iz ve bezt techno gabba.' He went on to enthuse about the hardcore sounds that 've will not find anyvere else in ve city.' We continued to smile politely. And then we wrote it down – because frankly, he was quite scary. Then we got drunk and danced badly to the best techno gabba in the city. Techno gabba, for the uninitiated, is the sort of hardcore, non-stop headache inducing techno best loved by scary German tourists. If you're a scary German tourist, you'll love this place. If you are being hounded by a scary German tourist, you won't.

■ ■ ■ The Level
24 Park Row (0117) 373 0473

Let me introduce you to The Level. Stylish clubbing has arrived in Bristol. The designers of the acclaimed E-Shed have remodelled the interior to resemble a retro airport lounge. Check out the silver sci-fi slouch sofas, then try saying 'silver sci-fi slouch sofas' after a pint or two of vodka. With a top of the range Thunder Ridge sound system

blasting out everything from soul to house, no corners have been cut. Nothing here is a compromise. Pure class.

■ ■ ■ The Lizard Lounge
Queens Road (0117) 949 7778

You know you shouldn't like this place, but you just can't help yourself. It's tacky and it knows it. So does everyone else. But no-one cares. Grab a partner and dance 'til you drop. Grab a tequila and drink 'til you drop. Pop into the Red Room. It's red. No class, no pretensions, no way you can fail to have a good time. Full of up-for-it students – especially on 'Mad For It' Mondays.

■ ■ ■ The Mandrake Club
8 Frogmore Street

A small venue, consisting of interlinked stone cellars. More of a late night bar than a club offering some decent deals on spirits. Although the décor is a bit nondescript, the building itself is around 400 years old. Perfect for scores of visiting historians then.

Flick through the papers

■ ■ New Trinity

Trinity Road, St Phillips (0117) 907 7119

A massive converted church – it's not your average club with comfy sofas and patterned carpets. Split into two levels and hosting trance nights from Time Gate and tech–trance from Sci-Ting. Think white gloves, glow sticks and a lot of sweat. Past promoters who have entertained the masses here include Ruff Neck, Mutant Dance and Species.

Jason, 18, Student

Nice Hair. Where do you show it off? Hatchet.
What about moshing? Inferno.
Where do you students go to get fed properly? Riverstation.
And what about purchasing clothes to compliment your barnet? BS8.
What's the best thing about the city? Its cosmopolitan nature.
And the worst? Meders (broadmeaders) and their regional dialect.
Not people with normal hair then...

■ ■ Nocturne

1 Unity Street (0117) 929 2555

Formerly the Silent Peach , and now a private members club. It was local heroes, Massive Attack, who decided that this is what the Bristol clubbing scene needed. There's a definite air of exclusivity, bordering on the pretentious, well, pretentious for Bristol anyway. It's not easy to become a member, but if you do get through the stringent selection policy, you'll only have to stump up £67 for a year's membership – compare that to a season ticket at Ashton Gate, and you'll realise what a bargain it is. It boasts the only sound system of its kind in the country with flat speakers covered in leather all dotted around the club. It's only open Wed-Sun, but you can drink until 2am and dance up to 6 in the morning. Now, hopefully, they'll give me that membership I've been waiting for all year.

■ ■ Po Na Na

Queens Road, Clifton (0117) 904 4445

It's a Moroccan themed club. Yes, another one. You should be well aware of the Po Na Na chain by now, so you'll know what to expect: draped ceilings, soft seating, the usual decent blend of hip hop, house, funk and breaks. Consistently popular, especially with people who like Moroccan themed clubs. And still no sign of any camels.

■ ■ The Rock

Frogmore Street (0117) 927 9227

Since its conception in December 2000, thousands of happy clubbers have passed through the doors and boy, have they got what they paid for. Sleek interiors and upholstery aside, it hasn't been a garden of roses for the super-club, but they've weathered the storm and the critics and have

top 5 for...
Pulling (Fussy)

1. Level
2. Creation
3. Dojo Lounge
4. Rock
5. Fez Club

gone from strength to strength with the oh so popular 'Scream' clubbing night every Friday. Residents Paul Conroy, The Saint and Dan Pearce guard the coveted decks with special and regular guests such as Pete Tong, Lisa Lashes and Boy George to name a few. The adopted door policy of 'No wankers and twats' ensures that lashed up townies keep away. Other nights see a range of pro- moters from 2 Kool for Skool – uniforms at the ready, the popular Boogie Wonderland and Glitterbug. Sundays sees the hot Sundissential West crew, with residents, Charlotte Birch and Ed Karney mixing up hard house anthems 'til 2am. With live bands at the start of the week and a dedicated stu- dent night (that's a night dedicated to stu- dents, not a night for dedicated students – Ed) on Thursday, it shuns the mainstream approach and dishes up breaks & beats, house and hip hop 'til 3am.

■ ■ ■ The Steamrock
14-15 King Street (0117) 922 6149/5

The Steamrock is a student only venue so if you ain't got your NUS card you'll be hound- ed out of the place. Beg, borrow or steal one and you'll be in for a decent night. The place has leopard skin walls. And in my book leopard skin walls pretty much guarantee an excellent night out. As with any student venue there's also shit loads of drink promos and cheesy chart music. Visit at the weekend to get a real feel for the place and while you're there take up the 100 shot challenge. Can you knock back 100 shots of beer in 100 minutes? Take my word for it – you can't. And it'll cost £6 to enter – so best just order a pint and check out the talent. Looking to get laid – this is easy pickings. If you go home alone from The Steamrock then you're either a social reject or Welsh.

■ ■ ■ Thekla
The Grove (0117) 929 3301

A converted merchant boat, permanently moored on Bristol's canal makes this a very unique and interesting club. Rumour has it that it's been sinking for years, but, much like Venice, it still seems to be keeping its head above water. And, thankfully, it doesn't just trade on the unusual surroundings. The

Best Nights

Jazz & Blues @ Bunch of Grapes, Tue & Thur.
House & Garage @ The Rock
Techno & Electronica/Trance @ New Trinity
Centre, 'Sci-Ting'
Soul & Funk @ The Fez, 'Solo Rhythms'
Indie @ Advisory, 'The Cooler'
Hip Hop & RnB @ The Level Club
World Music @ Tantric Jazz
Folk @ The Folkhouse
Drum&Bass @ Creation Club, 'Drive By'
Sixties, Mowtown, Northern Soul @ Thekla
Club, 'Espionage'
Rock @ The Fleece & Firkin
Classical & Opera @ Bristol Hippodrome
Pop & Rock @ Colston Hall
Metal/Alternative @ The Bierkeller
Student Night – Galaxy Student Dance
Party @ Creation Club

hekla turns out some quality sounds; drum
'n' bass on Fridays, and some cracking funk
t the weekends. Set on two levels, you can
get away from the music and even get hold
of some grub from the upstairs bar. Some
xcellent one-off nights covering every-
hing from jazz, funk and 60s complete the
ne up. Recommended.

■ ■ Vaultz
● Frogmore Street (0117) 9349076

he Frog and Toad is no more. Welcome, in
ts place, the Vaultz Bar & Club. As the name
uggests, (Vaultz – clever twist on vaults,
ee…) it's located in the basement area and

operates as a bar in the evening, and as a
club as the night wears on. Inside, the bar
area takes centre stage with the designated
dancefloor area in an L-shape set off from
the bar so there's no chance of any over
enthusiastic dancer smacking you in the
chops with a stray arm. Amusement-wise
there's a pool table and table football with
plenty of seating if you opt for a chat or
three-draw session on the plastic men. You
can also have a go at the Playstations or fruit
machine, but the latter might leave you
lighter so if you're a bit skint, take a peek
at the linked projector screen, which shows
music videos and is free. Better still, get
on the dancefloor and strut your funky
stuff to house and hip hop. Open Thur-Sat
5pm-2am.

■ ■ ■ The Works
15 Nelson Street (0117) 929 2658

Welcome to The Works. This is the place of
nightmares. With enough cheese to make a
gallon of fondue, a clientele with an average
IQ of 12 and insipid, uninspiring décor, it's no
wonder that everyone in here is so pissed.
You'd have to be blind drunk to even think
about going to The Works. Not everyone
agrees with us though, the place claims to
be the busiest club in the South West, so
don't take our word for it; stick on your white
tracksuit bottoms and check the place out
for yourself – but don't say you weren't
warned. Oh, and avoid the bogs unless you
have a thing about wading through the par-
tially digested contents of someone else's
stomach. Student Night: Tuesday.

RIZLA ✚ **It's what you make of it.**

club listings

For more up-to-date reviews, previews and listings check www.itchybristol.co.uk

All listings details are subject to change at short notice, and should therefore be used as a guide only

Club	Night	Price	Music		
MONDAY					
The Cooler	Advisory	Indie/Rock		£2/£3	10-2am
Creation	-	Promoters/Variable			9-3am
Evolution	Student night	Britpop/chart		£3/£4	9.30-2am
Fez Club	Rock Star	Hip Hop/R&B		£3	10-2am
Lakota	Student Grant	Commercial Chart		£1	9-2am
Steamrock	Student night	Cheesy Chart		£3	9.30-2am
Club Crème		lap/table dancing		-	9-2am
Queenshilling	-	house/mix		-	9-2am
TUESDAY					
Café Blue	Locus	drum&bass(student)		£3-£5	10-3am
The Cooler	Cheese Night	cheesy chart		£2/£3	10-2am
Creation	Galaxy student dance party	dance/party		£3	9-3am
Evolution	-	R&B/Dance		£3/£4	9.30-2am
The Fez	4-play	old skool/hip hop		£3	10-2am
Lakota	Sugar(student night)	funky disco		£1-£4	9-2am
The Works	Ignition(student night)	chart/dance		£2/£3	9-2am
Queenshilling	-	house/mix		-	9-2am
Club Crème	lap/table dancing	-			9-2am
WEDNESDAY					
Bierkeller	-	metal/indie/punk		£3.50-£4.50	8-2am
Blue Mountain	-	indie/funk/hip hop		£2/£3	10-2am
Café Blue	Indie Night	indie/pop		£3/£4	10-2am
The Cooler	Cool Salsa	salsa		£2.50-£3.50	8-2am
Creation	-	variable		£3-£6	9.30-2am
Evolution	Wedgies	cheesy chart		£2/£3	10-2am
Fez	Play Baby	grooves/funk/soul		£3	10-2am
Lakota	Lush	r&b / garage		£4/variable	9-2am
Level	-	D&B/House/Hip		£3-£7	9-2am
Steamrock	ibiza dance night	club anthems		£3.50	9.30-2am
Queenshilling	-	house/mix		-	9-2am
Club Crème	lap/table dancing	lap/table dancing		-	9-2am
THURSDAY					
Bierkeller	Immaculate 80's	chart/disco		£2/£3	9-2am
Blue Mountain	-	drum&bass		£5	10-2am
Café Blue	-	UK Garage/hip hop		£3-£5	10-3am
The Cooler	Technique	funk/D&B/beats		£2-£6	10-2am
Creation	Fly	hip hop/r&b/grooves		£4	10-3.30am
Evolution	Uncovered	dance anthems		£3/£4	10-2am

The Fez	Chique Boutique	r&b/hip hop/funk	£3	10-2am
Level	-	House/D&B/Hiphop	£3-£7	9-2am
The Mandrake	Generation X	Alternative	£2	10-2am
New Trinity	-	Trance/techno/beats	£5-£10	10-4am
The Steamrock	Salsa Night	latin/disco	£3/£4	7.30-2am
The Rock	Come Play (student night)	mix	£4	9.30-3am
The Vaultz	-	Chart/dance	£1.50	9-2am
The Works	Wired	club/party	£3/£4	9-2.30am
Queenshilling	-	House/mix	-	9-2am
Cub Crème	-	lap/table dancing	-	9-2am

FRIDAY

Bierkeller	Loaded	indie	£4/£5	10-3am
Blue Mountain	-	House/Underground	£5	10-2am
Café Blue	Mutiny/promoters	D&B	£3-£8	10-3am
The Cooler	Fridaze	funk/hip hop/soul	£2/£3	10-3am
Creation	Drive By/Promoters	drum&bass/R&B	£8/£10	10-4am
The Depot	-	D&B/funky techno	£5-£10	10-4am
Evolution	-	Commercial/Dance	£3-£5	9.30-4am
The Fez	Solo Rhythm	funk/soul/r&b	£4/£5	10-2am
Inferno	PlanetX / Eleviras	alt/goth	£4/£5	9-2am
Lakota	-	House/promoters	£5-£10	10-5am
Level	-	house/D&B/hiphop	£3-£7	9-2am
The Mandrake	-	Chart/Commercial	£2-£4	9-2.30am
New Trinity	-	Trance/Techno/beats	£5-£10	10-4am
The Rock	Scream	hrd house	£8-£15	9.30-4am
The Steamrock	Dynamite(student)	Chart/Commercial £4/£5	9.30-2am	-
Thekla	-	Drum &Bass/Hip Hop	£3-£7	9-2am
The Vaultz	-	Hard House	£4/£5	9-2am
The Works	Mischief	Anthems/Garage	£3-£5	9.30-2.30am
Queenshilling	-	House/mix	-	9-3am
Club Crème	lap/table dancing	lap/table dancing	-	9-2am

SATURDAY

Bierkeller	Oompah night	live band	£6.50	8-1am
Blue Mountain	Blowpop/promoters	breaks/hip hop	£7/£8	10-4am
Café Blue	Out of the blue	House	£5	10-4am
The Cooler	Ascention	soul/swing/hiphop	£4-£6	10-3am
Creation	Slinky	House	£8-£10	10-4am
The Depot	-	D&B/funky techno	£5-£10	10-4am
Evolution	Futura	chart/party	£4-£6	9.30-2am
The Fez	Casa Vibe	funky house	£5	9-3am
Inferno	Assylum	metal night	£4/£5	9-2am
Lakota	-	Hous/HipHop	£5-£10	10-6am
Level	-	r&b/hiphop/house	£3-£7	9-2am
The Mandrake	-	commercial chart	£2-£4	9-2.30pm
New Trinity	-	trance/beats	£5-£10	10-4am
The Steamrock	100shotclub	chart/party	£4-£6	9.30-2am
The Rock	Relax	disco	£8	9.30-3am
The Thekla	espionage/fruityantics	NorthernSoul/house	£3-£7	9/10-4am
The Vaultz	-	funk/hiphop	£4/£5	9-2am
The Works	Meltdown	club anthems	£4-£7	9-3am
Club Crème	lap/table dancing	lap/table dancing	-	9-2am
Queenshilling	-	House/mix	-	9-3am

shopping

www.itchybristol.co.uk

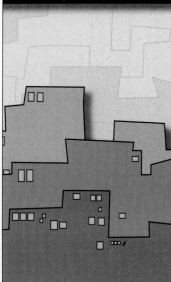

■ ■ Shopping Centres

■ ■ Broadmead
(0117) 977 1871

Broadmead – the central point of Bristol with all the big name stores that you've come to expect from any large city centre. Need new threads? Check out French Connection, Next, Envy, H&M, Gap and Wallis. Not after clothes? How about a visit to the Disney Store, Dixons, Carphone Warehouse or HMV. Largely uninspiring, it gives you the distinct feeling of 'haven't seen this somewhere before?' And chances are, you probably have.

■ ■ The Galleries
(0117) 929 0569

The Galleries – an indoor shopping centre housed in Broadmead. Take a look at the clothes in Kathy's Closet, Rogers & Rogers, Gap and Cassidy. Liven up your time here by paying a visit to the Gadget Shop. It all gets a bit tedious after a while, but at least they have the old favourites Waterstone's, HMV and Virgin to liven proceedings up.

■ ■ Clifton Village

A bustling village that oozes character and affluence, Clifton Village has tons of restaurants, wine merchants, delis, cafés, a supermarket and petrol station all crammed together in the space of a few streets. A great place to shop.

■ ■ Christmas Steps
(Off Colston Road/Perry Road)

You must visit the Christmas Steps if you're in Bristol shopping. The old streets are lined with quaint shops specialising in everything m musical instruments to stained glass. e Japanese would use several rolls of APS m before raving over the chippy at the ottom of the steps; watch the response hen they ask for a fork – very amusing. hCoffee.net – the internet café at the top is e only reminder that you are in the 21st ntury whilst the designer clock and light-g opposite set the time in a novel way. Well orth setting aside time for.

■ ■ Cribbs Causeway
117) 903 0303

rget about the 'shop until you drop' men-lity, this is more along the lines of 'drop efore you shop' as it takes an age to com-ute from the vast car parks to the mall. You n blame the Americans for introducing e out of town shopping experience to the its. We can't see the attraction of traipsing ound a mall looking at all the usual sus-ect chain stores, but if it's your thing then e Causeway will be paradise. The likes of ext, BHS, John Lewis, M&S, Dorothy Perkins d River Island can all be found here.

■ ■ Markets

■ ■ St Nicholas Markets
ff Corn Street

ome things never change and you get the npression that this place has probably ayed the same for centuries. A maze of uirky stalls offering hand made crafts, ome grown produce, glassware, knits and pair services. Oh and lest I forget, stalls sell-g CDs and records, which may have been a

bit too revolutionary back in 1743 when the market started out. Midweek, the local farmers set up organic fruit and veg stalls. Great stuff.

■ ■ Saturday Craft Market
Corn Street

The centre is often in need of brightening up and each Saturday the holders of around 70 stalls add that much-needed splash of colour to the streets. Browse through the stalls and imagine you're in Camden. Not quite the same, I know, but worth a look in all the same.

■ ■ Menswear

■ ■ Savoy Taylors Guild
76 Park Street (0117) 926 5511

A classy joint for suits and formal wear. It's definitely stuck out on a limb amidst the laid-back surfer places that line good old Park Street.

■ ■ Wired
30 Park Street (0117) 903 0942

Don't be surprised if you see some stylish Premier League footballers in here (although they won't play for either of the

Bristol teams). Evisu, Savage London, Armani, Stone Island and Duffer rule in this posh, but blokey shop. Walk in with a copy of FHM under your arm and feel at home.

■ ■ ■ Rollermania
Park Row (0117) 927 9981

Skaters and board freaks worship this place. If you need to replace trucks, wheels or buy that new video showing you da' moves you can't go wrong here. Two floors of software (clothes) and hardware. Tends to get obscenely packed on weekends with baby-faced youths. Upstairs stocks t-shirts, trainers by Globe, Sens, Axion including belts and hoodies. Downstairs stocks a comprehensive range of longboards and skateboards.

■ ■ ■ Women's Clothes

■ ■ ■ Cara
26 Park Street (0117) 925 7495

Bring your mother here and she'll be well impressed. Sells shoes by the likes of Camper, Rocket Dog and Red or Dead and clothes by Shelly's, Lacey's, Bronk, Palex and Cara.

■ ■ ■ City Dolls
59 Park Street (0117) 927 7307

Lie back and think of Newquay; this place is for all those surf chicks or fashion conscious beach dressers out there. O'Neill, Billabong, Rip Curl and Kanabeach are the most popular labels. Its presence is made on the Park Street strip with glitzy metal interior and cool glass head stands modelling all t' hats. Two floors of fashion for the bea' babes of Bristol.

■ ■ ■ DNA
24 Park Street (0117) 934 9173

Full on student type shop for those wh detest the smart tidy look but love the labels. Stocking Paul Frank and his monkey Fred Perry, Dusty Da Costa, Atari (the t-sh not the computer) and Dunlop. Look out f' their own brand goods – Plaything.

■ ■ ■ Jigsaw
80 Park Street (0117) 926 5775

If you're a mature girl you'll appreciate th place. Neatly pressed clothes in colour c' ordinated racks – very feng shui. The sho has a beach hut feel; all neutral colours ar swing style changing rooms.

■ ■ ■ Oasis
Cribbs Causeway (0117) 959 0111
Union Street (0117) 925 1572

Weekend shopping is like going to war ar Oasis is the front line, packed come Saturda

YOU'RE IN AN INTERVIEW

ernoon with panic-stricken girls on a per-t outfit mission. Oasis offers designer le at affordable prices, a fast enough turn-er to ensure you don't end up in the same sters as every other girl in your local and myriad of up-to-the-minute shoes and cessories. Everything you could ever need. nkly I'd move in if only they'd let me.

■ ■ Unisex Clothes Shops

■ ■ Alterior

Park Street (0117) 927 2514

cently relocated shop with a distinctive le and casual vibe. Stocking the Bristol sed Kuldesac T-shirts and hoodies. Also ls Bond, New Balance, Elk, Haze and the astie Boy'label, X-Large. A really chilled t store and a good place to pick up a pair Dunlops or a rather gorgeous shop assis-nt. Also exhibits work by local graffiti ists (who no doubt purchase their Belton plotov spray cans here).

■ ■ BS8

Park Street (0117) 930 4836

d fronted with a massive sign so you can't ss it. Move yo' ass into this maze of clothes d footwear outlets. The popular Road ans and Go Vicinity brand take up the ont section with the Naughty Girl skinny fit signs of the Custard brand – which are ry popular with students. Move back into x Boutique for more casual wear and beys for all your flares, American retro and ils of T-shirt prints. Upstairs is for the

blokes with Monkey Boy T-shirts and wait for it, Male Masseur – say no more. Down in the basement all trance and techno hippies will love the boot clobber of Swear and clothing by Space Tribe, Kiss The Future and Paranoid.

■ ■ Clothing Federation

56 Park Street (0117) 929 9889

The place to come for a cheap Friday night T-shirt that you can spill beer on and puke down without worrying about it. Selling thumb rings and cheap jewellery bits for those body mutilations.

■ ■ Cooshti

57 Park Street (0117) 929 0850

Attractive staff and cool labels crammed into two rooms. Expect to whip out your visa and quiver. Labels stocked include Replay, Diesel, Hope and Glory, Miss Sixty and Duffer and a good collection of footwear, bags, toi-letries and other accessories. One of the trendiest shops on Park Street.

DON'T GET INTIMIDATED BY THEIR EYE CONTACT

■ ■ ■ Mapatasi
71 Park Street (0117) 934 9444

A well thought out store with a wide selection of labels from FCUK to Rude and Evisu. It may be expensive, but it stocks some of the coolest, most exclusive labels around from One True Saxon to Denime and Seal Kay. Also sells some quality jewellery and a selection of shoes and trainers. Desirable, but pricey, for those who know their stuff.

■ ■ ■ Uncle Sam's
54 Park Street (0117) 929 8404

Park Street's only second hand shop for all you retro kids and those who just can't let go of decades past. Some very cool leather jackets and bowling shirts as well as Kitsch-u-like vinyl bags. Plays some fantastic music to encourage hours of browsing. If the Dude came to Bristol, you'd find him here with a White Russian firmly in hand.

■ ■ ■ Surf/Adventure Sports Shops – Unisex

■ ■ ■ Shark Bite
68 Park Row (0117) 929 9211

How cool is this place? Beach hut style with bamboo roof, wooden plinth rails and leop-ard skin changing rooms with videos of su and snowboarding competitions playir constantly. Two floors stocking rucksac body and surfboards, whilst snowboards c be hired out. The usual suspects are for sale Quiksilver, Reef, Billabong and Mambo.

■ ■ ■ White Stuff
64 Queens Road (0117) 929 0100

A bit off the beaten track, so if you're lost, it next to Karen Millen – which is only usef advice if you know where Karen Millen Check out the surfboard style lights for real surprise. Unisex beachwear for laid bac lazy days or nights. More discerning 'scruf come here than long-haired kids who like say 'dude' a lot.

■ ■ ■ Footwear

■ ■ ■ The Boot Room
22 Park Street (0117) 922 5455

Shelly's, Buffalo, Fornarina, Acupuncture an a large selection of seriously sexy boots. spacious shop for the foxy and funky. Kitte heels a go go.

■ ■ ■ soletrader
8 Broadmead Gallery, Broadmead
(0117) 929 1122

A veritable haven of smart shoes and eve trendier trainers. Situated on the ground flo level of the Gallery, there's no stairs, so yo can save your feet, whilst you shop for you footwear. With an excellent range of desig for men, women and even children, mak

"OI, WHAT ARE YOU LOT STARING AT!?"

sure you take your pick from their vast selection. There's smart shoes and boots from the likes of Hugo Boss, French Connection, Timberland, Rockport, Patrick Cox and Ted Baker. Or relax your feet into cool but comfy trainers coming from Diesel, Buffalo, Puma, Nike, Adidas, Vans, Converse, Acupuncture and Etnies, amongst others. With an almost endless source of options, don't just take our word for it, find out for yourself.

◼️◼️ Stepping Out
Broadmead (0117) 927 3555
Footwear with attitude – or so they say. Full of panic-stricken girls on the hunt for the perfect strappy number and disappointed farmers complaining about the lack of wellies on sale. The likes of Milano Moda, Gardone, Ebony and Rebel labels all sold here. Go elsewhere farmers, there's nothing for you here.

◼️◼️ Funky and Cool Shops

◼️◼️ B-Delicious

2 Triangle South, Clifton (0117) 929 1789
Bristol's only specialist bead shop, and boy are they popular with the students and creative types. Hair clips, accessories, sequins, feathers, trims, body and hair jewellery, and of course thousands of beads. If you know what you want they'll design and make it for you.

◼️◼️ The Gadget Shop
The Galleries & Cribbs Causeway (0800) 783 8343
Thank God for The Gadget Shop. After all where else would you go to do your Christmas and birthday shopping when you're looking for something a little bit different from bubble bath or pants and socks? Gadget Shop, we salute you.

cards
gifts
wrap
xmas
valentines
mothers day
fathers day
birthdays

75 Queens Road Clifton Bristol BS8 1QP

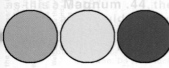

POINTBLANK

be different...

■ ■ Daxx Communications

88 Park Street (0117) 930 4304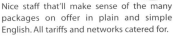

Nice staff that'll make sense of the many packages on offer in plain and simple English. All tariffs and networks catered for.

■ ■ Point Blank

75 Queens Road (0117) 904 6690

Lara Croft, prepare to meet your match. Point Blank have a super babe in here – check out the back wall. A padded mental asylum of crazy gifts, cards, accessories and gadgets that you just won't find anywhere else. We like the lighters and rather inventive range of contemporary playthings. Not a micro-scooter in sight.

■ ■ Repsycho

85 Gloucester Road (0117) 983 0007

This is one cool shop. Selling retro clothes, shoes and music, all tossed out by your gran and worn by the dudes who like to relive the 60s and 70s. Check out the majorly cool 70s furniture. We could waste hours in here. Shagadelic, as some tossers still like to say.

■ ■ Deck Out Your Pad

■ ■ Guild

(Bristol Guild of Applied Art)
70 Park Street (0117) 926 5548

Do you appreciate the finer things in life? If you do then you should make your way to Guild. There's three floors to trawl around; glassware by Paul Costelloe, Wedgwood ceramics, practical kitchenware as well as toys, cards, crafts, prints, frames, bags and accessories for the home. Check out the Guild delicatessen as you leave, but it's gotta be said, the Alessi orange squeezer is a winner for me.

■ ■ Mart
Jacobs Road, Hotwells (07979) 352505
Super cool art deco and contemporary glassware, light shades, metal works and jewellery. Loads of original pieces from local designers. Lives up to its manifesto: art is for everyday, everybody and every pocket; the goods and prices certainly reflect this.

■ ■ Robin Purpose Furniture
Jacobs Road, Hotwell (0117) 929 1088
Need a cabinet, mirror or sideboard? Robin's your man. With his workshop and showroom in one shop you are assured of quality crafts and service. No flat pack crap here, just quality handcrafted furniture. Nice one, Robin.

■ ■ Scooter Shops

■ ■ Scooters Direct
Lewis Mead, Town Centre (0117) 925 7666
Your local scooter and accessories shop. Look nifty on a Vespa and pretend to be that cheeky chappie Jamie Oliver for a day – just don't forget your trademark yellow sweater. All other makes and models are sold such as Italjet, Piaggio, Aprilia and Peugeot. Ask the friendly staff for advice and assistance.

■ ■ Music Shops

■ ■ Backyard Records
31 St. Stephen's Street (0117) 926 4968
Specialists in hip hop, and the place you'll usually find all the local DJs hanging out – and that's a recommendation, not a warning.

■ ■ Bangbang Records
80 Colston Street (0117) 922 7377
Grey and orange music shop stocking vinyl. There's a Rizla machine if you need a puff – nice touch. Experts in ambient, funk, US & UK garage, progressive techno, house, trance, hard house and funky house. And three decks to sample the goods.

■ ■ Breakbeat Culture
60 Park Row, Clifton (0117) 929 7372
Basement vinyl shop. Special stockists of drum 'n' bass and hip hop. Friendly service with sample decks and if you can't find what you're looking for, ask nicely and they might order it for you. Check out the itchy card deal for discounts.

■ ■ Eat The Beat
11 St Nicholas Street (0117) 925 1691
Vinyl shop and milk bar in one. Two floors with four listening posts and decks to get jiggy with. Jungle, funk, reggae; you name it, they stock it.

■ ■ Fopp Records
Park Street (0117) 945 0685
The Fopp logo can be seen from anywhere on Park Street. They exploded onto the

koko.com

street earlier this year, and they've already built up a huge following. Big in all respects, stocking every conceivable CD in most genres and a range of vinyl, books and videos, all at bargain prices.

■■■ HMV
19-21 Broadmead (0117) 929 7467
Cribbs Causeway

Opening a new branch of the massive chain store in Cribbs Causeway is bound to please the masses that shop in the precinct. Both stores sell the most comprehensive range of CDs, videos, and music magazines. If you can't find what you want then they'll order it for you.

■■■ Imperial Music
58 Park Street (0117) 987 9700
Several listening posts and decks, stocking a

range of vinyl and second hand CDs. A lar selection of indie, rock, jazz, funk, electro ca, dance, hip hop, drum 'n' bass and techn Diverse and eclectic, catering for all taste Quality.

■■■ Onyx Music
54 Park Street (0117) 929 0419

Cheap CDs proclaims the window display we get the message. Stocking all the usu CDs, from chart to Marilyn Manson. Mass of Goth T-shirts are suspended from the ce ing to pull in the black nail varnish cre Korn, Incubus and most things morbid.

■■■ Rooted Records
9 Gloucester Road, Bishopston
(0117) 907 4372

One of the few record shops out of tow that's worth a mention. The Rooted boys ce

WHATEVER TURNS YOU ON *Virgin* megastores

tainly know their stuff when it comes to vinyl especially drum 'n' bass and hip hop. This unique shop is decked out with four listening posts and graffiti. They offer a discount to most and adopt a policy of no attitude, just gratitude to their punters who come back to this outlet. Stocking other music genres such as techno, house, UK garage, electronica, old school, breakbeat, dub and roots. If you can't find what you want, the boys will help you out – just ask.

■ ■ Virgin Megastore

The Cribbs Causeway (0117) 950 9600
The Galleries, Broadmead (0117) 929 7798
A veritable music mecca, selling CDs, DVDs and vinyl. Also stocks Playstation 2 and Gameboy accessories as well as a huge selection of magazines and the (ahem) itchy guide.

■ ■ Bookshops

■ ■ Blackwell's

89 Park Street (0117)927 6602
Over five floors of written material and one of the best coffee shops in Park Street.
Coldharbour Lane (0117) 965 2573
No escaping the books, students. The Blackwell's treatment condensed to fulfil all your paperback needs.

■ ■ Waterstone's

27-29 College Green (0117) 925 0511
33 Lower Mall Cribbs Causeway
(0117) 950 9813
11a Union Gallery, Broadmead
(0117) 925 2274
Bristol Uni, Tyndall Ave (0117) 925 4297
Stocking all the bestsellers and much, much more. Book signings, artwork and a café, plus they stock a super little guide to Bristol, the name escapes me, but it'd make the perfect stocking filler for all your mates.

■ ■ WHSmith

24 Clifton Down Shopping Centre,
Whiteladies Road (0117) 973 5063
2-4 Clifton Village (0117) 973 3255
The Galleries, Broadmead (0117) 925 2152
Cribbs Causeway (0117) 950 9525
Comprehensive chain store that stocks everything you need for your pencil case, as well as a huge selection of magazines and books to relax and unwind with. Plus... you guessed it, the itchy guides as well.

entertainment

www.itchybristol.co.uk

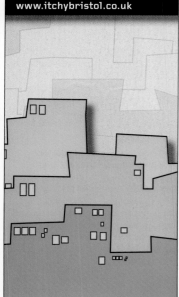

Cinemas

ABC
Whiteladies Road (0117) 973 3640
At the time of going to press, ABC is threatened with closure, so assuming the ABC is still with us, you can always catch the latest big thing or something a bit more off the wall if you so desire.
Adults £3.75 after 6pm. NUS £3.20

The Cube
King Square (0117) 907 4191
Small but perfectly formed, The Cube appears to be in a state of denial over Hollywood, and steadfastly ignores blockbusters. Frequent lectures and discussion groups amid a steady supply of fantastically strange cult movies.
Adults £3

The Odeon
Union Street, Broadmead 0870 505 0007
Don't risk the 'standard' seating – once you've got your arse wedged in, you're there for life. Hollywood films all the way.
Adults £3.20

Orpheus
**Northumbria Drive, Henleaze
(0117) 962 1644**
You have to love a place that has 'Bargain Tuesdays'. There are three small screens, and the seats are so cheap that we really have no idea how they make any money.
Adults £3.50, NUS £2.50

Showcase
Avonmeads, St Philips (0117) 972 3800
Fourteen screens, reclining chairs, a bar and

all the sweets you can eat. However, getting to St. Philips (where?) will cost you more than the film, and the length of the recorded message is better measured in geological periods than minutes.
Adults £3.50

■ ■ Warner Village
Cribbs Causeway (0117) 950 0050
Loads of leg room and seats, but low on character.
Adults £5.20, NUS £3.90

■ ■ Watershed Media Centre
Canon's Road (0117) 925 3845
Opposite the Arnolfini, and very similar in look, though to be fair the Watershed has more atmosphere. Filled with arty, alternative types enthusing over arty, independent films from Bulgaria, sculptures that make you want to think of other, more pleasant things, photographic darkrooms, film studies students posing on the stairs – you know the drill by now, surely?
Adults £4.20, NUS £3

■ ■ Theatres

■ ■ Alma Tavern
Alma Vale Road (0117) 973 5171
Alma Tavern neatly combines beer and theatre in one tidy little package. The box office opens an hour before each performance.

■ ■ Arnolfini
Narrow Quay (0117) 929 9191
Arnolfini is the centre of culture. The cinema

doubles as a theatre, and shows independent arty films, though you can also catch Hollywood classics. The perfect place to hang out with drama students and budding thespians calling each other daaaarling.

■ ■ Bristol Hippodrome
St Augustine's Parade (0870) 607 7500
Bristol Hippodrome usually shows music-based stuff, which can be anything from musicals to opera to ballet. Sadly, the quality varies as much as the genre. The bar doubles as an extortion racket, but if you're smart you'll wait for possible returns for cheaper ticket prices.

■ ■ Bristol Old Vic
King Street (0117) 987 7877
Famous all over the country, The Old Vic is best known for fantastic Shakespeare. All the productions set very high standards and attract big names, both on stage and in the audience. The student discounts are whopping, and the New Vic (downstairs) is the place to go if you fancy something experimental.

top 5 for...
Late Drinking

1. Arc Bar
2. E-Shed
3. Revolution
4. The Park
5. Ether

■ ■ QEH
Jacob's Well Rd (0117) 925 0551/987 7877
Often host to small local companies, the variety of drama at QEH has to be experienced to be believed; take a look at their season program on itchybristol.co.uk if you don't believe me. Owned by QEH school, so take steps to avoid the hordes of kids strapped down to watch The Cherry Orchard.

■ ■ The Tobacco Factory
Raleigh Road, Southville (0117) 902 0345
Like The Old Vic, best known for quality straight drama. Given the quality of last year's Hamlet, it's hard to see why The Tobacco Factory isn't as well known as it might be. A little off the beaten track, but easily as good as theatres three times the size in London.

■ ■ Wickham Theatre
Contocks Close, Woodland Road (0117) 928 7834
Like the Winston and Lady Windsor, the frankly minute Wickham is owned by the University. So experimental you can almost see the test tubes, this is a theatre that really tries to nurture talent, so you might be the first to see something really special. Can be astoundingly brilliant or embarrassingly bad, often in the same performance.

■ ■ Live Music Venues

■ ■ Bierkeller
All Saints St, The Pithay (0117) 926 8514
A truly eclectic music venue. As well as the metal, punk, goth, industrial line-up, you'll find an 80s, indie and Oompah band night. Shouldn't work, but it does.

■ ■ Bunch of Grapes
Denmark Street (0117) 987 0500
A traditional pub in the heart of Bristol with a fine reputation for live jazz and blues. Live acts perform on Tuesdays, Thursdays and Fridays.

■ ■ The Black Swan
Stapleton Road, Easton (0117) 939 3334
Serving up a hefty dose of ska, reggae, dub, roots and culture bands to the masses. A local pub by day and a live music venue at night, it has a rough and ready appeal. Come here to appreciate the music, not the décor.

■ ■ Colston Hall
Colston Street (0117) 922 3686
Bristol's attempt at matching Wembley Arena, this is the premier concert hall in the city. Let's be honest, it's not Wembley and it

IT'S THE DREAM JOB.

never will be, but it has brought some big names, such as Super Furry Animals, Wheatus, Stereo MCs, Jack Dee and Van Morrison to the city. Check itchybristol.co.uk for listings and details.

■ ■ ■ The Fleece
12 St. Thomas Street (0117) 929 9008
One of the notable live music venues in the South West, which has recently re-emerged from a massive makeover. It's one of those formidable Firkin pubs, but don't let that put you off. Improved facilities such as air conditioning, monitors and a lighting rig are now in place. With enough room for 400, they're expecting the crowds – and laying on an impressive programme of events and gigs to ensure it's busy every night.

■ ■ ■ Fiddlers
Willway St, Bedminster (0117) 987 3403
Fiddlers is a well respected music venue with plenty to shout about. Expect to see plenty of brass and Latin grooves here, with

live sets from all corners of the globe. Bristol based soul band, Tailfeather play here regularly, along with rock tribute band Whole Lotta Led. Check itchybristol.co.uk for listings and details.

■ ■ ■ The Old Duke
King Street (0117) 927 7137
Even your dad will know about this place. A jazz pub with a history of hosting artists and names as long as the Severn Bridge. Pulling a mixture of students and crooners alike.

■ ■ ■ The Rock
Frogmore Street (0117) 927 9227
Superclub-cum-music venue that has plans to host the best bands on the circuit. The venue is a plush affair and the bands are already queuing at the door to get a slot. Expect to see the likes of Ash, Faithless, Groove Armada and other big names topping the bill at this popular night spot.

■ ■ Severn Shed
The Grove (0117) 925 1212
A new addition to the live music scene that is showcasing jazz and world music artists of the highest calibre. At all other times the venue acts as a bar-cum-restaurant. Check itchybristol.co.uk for details.

■ ■ Tantric Jazz Café
39-41 St Nicholas Street (0117) 940 2304
An intimate candlelit jazz bar in the centre of town. Combining live music and DJs from the jazz spheres. Fronted by top West

BUT YOU DON'T WANT TO LOOK DESPERATE.

Country jazz DJ, Tony Clark, and resident band Jazzeera with an ever-changing line-up of artists and genres. Expect Eastern jazz, North African soul and Brazilian roots. Respected and well worth a visit.

Helen, 27, Sales Consultant

And your favourite bar is...
Ha Ha's.
How about a club? Watershed.
Where do you munch tasty morsels?
Browns, Vinchenzo's.
Where do you get your outfits?
Broadmead - Miss Selfridge, French Connection.
Best thing about Bristol?
So much variety.
And the worst?
Too messy & tatty, chewing gum on the pavements.

■ ■ ■ Bristol Uni – Anson Rooms
Queen's Road (0117) 954 5830
Hotline 0870 44 44 400

Another term starts and so does a hot line-up of gigs to boot. Expect to see the likes of Mercury Rev, Mogwai, Turin Brakes, Shed Seven and Divine Comedy. Ring the ticket hot line or check itchybristol.co.uk for listings and details.

■ ■ ☐ Comedy

■ ■ ■ The Bristol Comedy Pub
117-119 Stokes Croft (0117) 903 0796

Check out the back room for live music, comedy and theatre performances. A ticket will set you back anything from £2-£3 upward.
Tue-Sat 5pm-1am, Mon 5pm-11pm,
closed Sun
Food Served: 5pm-12.30am Tue-Sat

■ ■ ■ The Bunch Of Grapes
Denmark Street (0117) 987 0500

Sunday sees the BOG comedy night with local and up-and-coming acts keeping the masses entertained from 7.30pm.
Mon-Sat 11.30am-2.30pm, 5-11pm, Sun
12-2.30pm, 6-10.30

■ ■ ■ Jesters
140-142 Cheltenham Road
(0117) 909 6655

Court the jester and he'll give you a rib tickling time. One of the respectable landmarks in Bristol and placing Cheltenham Road on the map. They attract raw talent from local and national corners with weekly stand-up slots and the new and improved World Of Cheese night, where you're expected to dress like an idiot. Dancing like your dad is officially cool and if you dress for the occasion, the 'stoopid' people will get a quid knocked off entry.
7.30pm-12am Mon, 10pm-2am Tue,
7.30pm-1am Wed.
(Nights and prices vary so phone for details)

SO DON'T APPLY FOR IT.

■ ■ ■ Hen & Chicken –
The Comedy Station
210 North St, Bedminster (0117) 922 3683
Situated in the suburb of Bedminster, The Comedy Station puts this average boozer on the map. Part of the Punch retail group, it plays host to comedy talent from the South West. The pub is up for a refurb at some point in the near future, but for now you'll have to make do with the less than extravagant décor. Upstairs, the venue can hold up to 120 with a bar, dancefloor and raised stage where the comedians perform. Popular names such as Richard Norton, Justin Lee Collins and Geoff Whitting can be seen here. Definitely one to check out, so log on to the itchy website for listings, ticket prices and updates
Fri, Sat & Sun nights 8.45pm-11pm

■ ■ ■ Bowling

■ ■ ■ Bowl Plex
**Aspects Leisure Complex, Kingswood
(0117) 961 0000**
Interactive video games, dancefloors with resident DJs, a late licensed bar and restaurant and American pool. Oh yes, and also bowling – all 24 lanes of it.
Open 7 days a week 9.30 'til late
1 game, Adults £3.45 Children £2.45

■ ■ ■ Megabowl

Brunel Way, Ashton Gate (0117) 953 8538
Arcade games, pool, indoor adventure golf, 35 bowling lanes... you get the picture. Keep the ungrown people amused by sending them to 'Planet Kids' – the soft play area. A comprehensive, fun night out for peanuts. (Worth going just to see peanuts on a night out).
Mon-Fri 12pm-11pm, Sat, Sun 10am-1pm
1 Game Adults £4.75 Children £4.25

■ ■ ■ Casinos

■ ■ ■ Grosvenor Casino
266 Anchor Road (0117) 929 2932
7-9 Triangle South (0117) 926 4693

■ ■ ■ Ladbroke Regency Casino
Redcliffe Way (0117) 921 3189

■ ■ ■ Climbing/Paintball/Skating

■ ■ ■ Bristol Climbing Centre
**St Werburghs Church, Mina Road
(0117) 941 3489**
Housed in a converted church, so if your little angels really have no hope of taking the easier stairway to heaven, try the wall and rope method and rest assured that at least in here there is no fiery furnace to greet them if they fail.
Mon-Fri 10am-10pm, Sat & Sun 10am-6pm
Instruction Course £35; after that £1
joining fee and £5 admission

...EVERYONE WELCOME

TENPIN BOWLING
LICENCED BARS
WIMPY DINERS
AMERICAN POOL
AMUSEMENT AREAS
QUASAR
AND SO MUCH MORE*

TO FIND YOUR NEAREST MEGABOWL VISIT OUR WEBSIT
OR CALL TALKING PAGES FREE ON 0800 600 900

*Facilities vary at each Megabowl

MEGABOWL

www.megabowl.co.uk

■ ■ ■ Bristol Ice Rink
Frogmore Street (0117) 929 2148
Mon-Fri 10.30-3.30, Sat & Sun 10.30-12.30
Prices start at £4.60 with skate hire

■ ■ ■ Skate 'n' Ride
Avon Street (0117) 907 9995
It's a huge indoor skate and BMX park ideal for adolescents with energy to burn. Remember, it's customary to leave at least a small part of flesh clinging to the pipes or track.
Mon-Fri 10am-10pm, Sat & Sun10am-12pm
£3.50 for 3 hours weekend, £3 week, non-members £1.50 extra
£5 annual membership

■ ■ ■ Thornbury Paintball Fields
Thrumps Wood, Eastwood Park, Thornbury, Gloustershire (01454) 851 134
Violence under the guise of entertainment – we love it. It has everything necessary for a truly awesome battle: 25 acres of woodland, a 50ft natural ravine, camo nets, paint bullets and guns that will fire at 6 shots a second.
£15 including full kit, 100 paintballs and lunch, £7 per extra 100 paintballs
Average cost for a day: £35-£40
Open 9.30-4.30

■ ■ ■ Snooker/Pool

■ ■ ■ Riley's Snooker Hall
15 Queens Road (0117) 929 4295
10am-11.30pm Mon-Thu,
10am-12am Fri-Sun

■ ■ ■ Carlton Snooker Club
20 Easton Road (0117) 955 3137
Open 24 hours serving food, tea, coffee and soft drinks, seven days a week

■ ■ ■ Sport

■ ■ ■ Bristol City FC
Ashton Gate
(0117) 963 0630/966 6666
The rivalry between the two Bristol clubs is immense with the red and whites of City usually coming out on top. Not quite Premiership material, but they try bless 'em.

■ ■ ■ Bristol Rovers FC
Memorial Stadium, Horfield
(0117) 924 7474
The Welsh motto of 'As long as we beat the English' has been somewhat altered to 'as long as we beat City'. For the Blue and Whites, that's all that matters – it's good to see standards haven't dropped.

■ ■ ■ Bristol Rugby Union Club
Memorial Stadium (0117) 908 5500
Will never quite match the success of their neighbours Bath, but their strength lies in propping up the Premiership table. Someone has to do it.

■ ■ Strip Clubs

■ ■ Club Crème
46 West Street, St Phillips
(07967) 251 398
Great looking birds with no clothes on.
Sounds terrible, doesn't it?
9pm-2am Mon-Sat, closed Sun

■ ■ Museums & Art Galleries

■ ■ Bristol Industrial Museum
Princes Wharf, Wapping Road
(0117) 925 1470
Just down the dock from the Maritime
Heritage Centre, the Industrial Museum con-
tains all manner of weird and wonderful
things, from a life size replica of Concorde's
cockpit to the world's first holiday caravan.
There's also an exhibition charting Bristol's
role in the slave trade.
10am-5pm Apr-Oct Sat-Wed, closed Thu &
Fri, Nov-Mar Sat & Sun only.
Free admission

■ ■ City Museum & Art Gallery
Queens Road (0117) 922 3571
Next door to the Wills Building, the City
Museum houses all things historical, including art and natural history, in the glass cases
that we're all familiar with from school trips.
There are kids activities, a gift shop, café, regular lectures and tours; the occasional visiting exhibits sometimes have an admission
fee, but it's usually a token gesture.
10-5 seven days a week
Free admission

■ ■ Ginger Gallery
84-86 Hotwells Road (0117) 929 2527
A mixed bunch really. Exhibitions change
regularly and include limited edition etch-
ings, lithographs, screen prints by British and
International Artists, contemporary paintings, ceramics, sculpture, jewellery, photog-
raphy and turned wood. Something for
everyone, but if you're interested in all of
them you're a freak.
Tue-Fri 10-4.45, Sat 10-5

■ ■ Royal West of England Academy
Queens Road (0117) 973 5129
At the time of going to press the beautiful
exterior is undergoing a major facelift, so
expect it to be looking shiny and new.
There's an impressive permanent collection
and a range of visiting exhibitions. A smashing way to spend a rainy day.
10-5.30 Mon-Sat, 2-5 Sun
Free admission

▪▪▪ SS Great Britain
Great Western Dock, Gas Ferry Road
(0117) 929 1843

Yet another of Isambard Kingdom Brunel's leftovers, this was the first propeller-driven iron ship to cross the Atlantic, built right here in the city a hundred and fifty years ago. She was a bit of a hit at the time, and led to the building of ocean liners like Titanic and the Lusitania. Now restored, she's a bit off the beaten track, but history doesn't get much more interesting than this. Occasionally cluttered with school trips.

10-4 winter, 10-5 summer
Adult £6.25, Senior Citizen £5.25, Child
£3.75, Family £16.50

▪▪ Days Out and Attractions

▪▪▪ Bristol Uni Botanic Garden
Bracken Hill, North Road, Leigh Woods
(0117) 973 3682

Part of several conservation and research programs, Bracken Hill is home to over 4,500 plant species. This is the perfect place to forget that you live in a big dirty city full of cars (even the sound of the motorway barely filters through the trees). There are small, perfectly formed formal gardens, experimental beds filled with medicinal plants and herbs, greenhouses and a wilderness of tiny rambling paths. It's restful, quiet, utterly gorgeous, lovingly cared for and totally free (in fact, for a measly tenner, you can become a Friend and have your own key for the weekend).

9-5 Mon-Fri, closed wknds and public hols.
Free admission

▪▪▪ Bristol Zoological Gardens
Gutherie Road Clifton (0117) 973 8951

Packed with families and animals in equal measure, there's enough here to keep you occupied for a whole day, which is probably why it costs so much.

9-6 seven days a week, animal houses open
'til 5pm
Adults £8.40, Students £7.40, Children
£4.80, Fri – senior citizens £3.70

▪▪▪ Explore @ Bristol
Harbourside (0117) 915 1000

None of your stand-off-don't-touch-me nonsense here. Everything is strictly interactive and multi-media, including the IMAX cinema (0117 915 5000) and state of the art planetarium. There are four zones, and the much-hyped Wildscreen-at-Bristol, which features a tropical rainforest with free-flying birds and butterflies. A bit pricey to visit every day, but if you've got kids visiting you, this will keep them quiet for hours.

10-6 seven days a week
Family ticket for Explore £19. Adult for
Explore £6.50, Adult for Wildscreen £6.50.
Concessions available.

useful info

www.itchybristol.co.uk

■ ■ ■ Travel

■ ■ ■ Airport
Bristol International Airport
....0870 1212 747

■ ■ ■ Buses
Airport Bus Link 0870 1212 747

First Bristol Buses
Badgerline, City Line, Streamline & Durbin
Customer Care Line ....(0117) 941 2525
Enquiries 0870 608 2608

National Express 08705 80 80 80

Night-Flyers ....(0117) 922 4454
Buses through the night every Friday and
Saturday from midnight until 6am in the
morning. The hourly buses connect at the
centre allowing you to make cross-city journeys. Tickets cost just £1.50 for all journeys.

Traveline 0870 608 2608
Bus services in Bristol and Bath

■ ■ ■ Park and Ride
A4 Bath Road...........................(0117) 922 3769
Long Ashton ....(0117) 968 8114

■■■ Car Hire

Avis
24 hour Reservations 0870 60 60 100
Bristol Airport..............................01275 473 533
Multi Storey Car Park, Rupert Street
....(0117) 929 2123
Network Rental UK ....(0117) 926 1205
Patchway Service Station, Gloucester Road
....01454 620 911

Europcar
The Triangle, Berkley Pl. ....(0117) 925 3839
Bristol Airport.............................01275 474 623

Hertz
Albert Cres, St Phillips ....(0117) 977 9777
Bristol Airport.............................01275 472 807

■■■ Scooters

Scooter Direct
Lewis Mead, Town Centre ....(0117) 925 7666
Scooters and accessories.

■■■ Van/Car Hire

Budget
The Huntsman Garage, Westerleigh Road,
Downend ....(0117) 915 9636

Kenning
59 Hartcliffe Way ....(0117) 966 2296

■■■ Taxis

Ace Taxis ....(0117) 9777 477 / 977 4777
British Cab Company ....(0117) 925 1111
Bristol District Taxis ....(0117) 965 2222
Domestic Cabs ....(0117) 909 9419
Eagle Cabs Ltd ....(0117) 923 2626 / 924 1414

■■■ Trains

National Rail Enquiries 08457 48 49 50

Traveline Public Transport Info
....0870 608 2 608

■■■ Travellers with Disabilities

Dial-a-Ride ....(0117) 959 0700

■■■ Tourist Information

Bristol Tourist Information Centre,
The Annexe @ Bristol, Harbourside

Bristol Tourist Board ....(0117) 926 0767

Waterbuses/Ferry Boat Service Enquiries
Welsh Back ....(0117) 927 3416
A round trip waterbus service provides daily
passenger and morning commuter services
from the historic harbour everyday from
April to September and at weekends
throughout the winter. Fares start at £1 for
adults and 60p for children.

Bristol Packet Boat Trips
Gas Ferry Road ....(0117) 926 8157

 koko.com

There's better things to spend money on.

Don't waste it on travel.

If you're under 26 or a student save £££'s on travel with a Young Persons' Discount Coachcard. Cards cost £9 and save you up to 30% off already low fares all year. Register online to receive special offers throughout the year.

For journey planning, tickets and coachcards
visit **GoByCoach**.com or call 08705 80 80 80

Check online for details.
Coach services depart from Marlborough Street, Bus Station, Bristol.

■ ■ Accommodation

Prices are per person bed and breakfast, based on two sharing

■ ■ Expensive

■ Holiday Inn Crowne Plaza
Crowne Plaza Victoria St (0117) 976 9988
Week £81.50 Weekend £39

■ ■ Bristol Marriot Hotel
College Green (0117) 925 5100
Week £82.50 Weekend £45

■ ■ Thistle Bristol
Broad Street (0117) 929 1645
Week/Weekend £81.50

■ ■ Mid Price Range

■ ■ The Berkley Square
15 Berkley Square (0117) 925 4000
Week £58.50 Weekend £42.50

■ ■ City Inn
Temple Way (0117) 925 1001
Week/Weekend £47

■ ■ Clifton Hotel
St Pauls Road, Clifton (0117) 973 6882
Week/Weekend £42

■ ■ Budget

■ ■ Basca House
19 Broadway Roads (0117) 942 2182
Week/Weekend £22.50

■ ■ Bristol City Centre Travel Inn
The Haymarket (0117) 9100 600
Week/Weekend £28

■ ■ Hostels

■ ■ Bristol Backpackers
17 Stephen's Street, City Centre
(0117) 925 7900
£12.50 a night

■ ■ YHA – Bristol
14 Narrow Quay (0117) 922 1659
£12.50 a night

■ ■ Apartments
Victoria Street (0117) 973 3344
Luxury short stay serviced apartments provide an alternative to hotel accommodation. Prices start at £50+VAT per night.

■ ■ University Accommodation

■ ■ The Hawthorns
Woodland Road, Clifton (0117) 954 5900
Close to the popular Park Street and the West End shopping area it offers budget student accommodation during the summer.

■ ■ Modelling Agencies

■ ■ Prolific Model Management
For models who are interested in registering with Profile please call their information line on 0906 641 1944 or call (0117) 922 0346 for all other information and details.

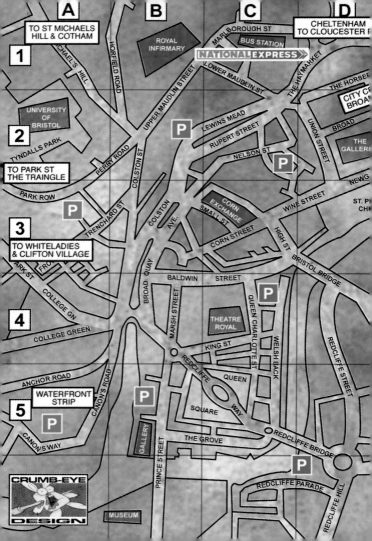

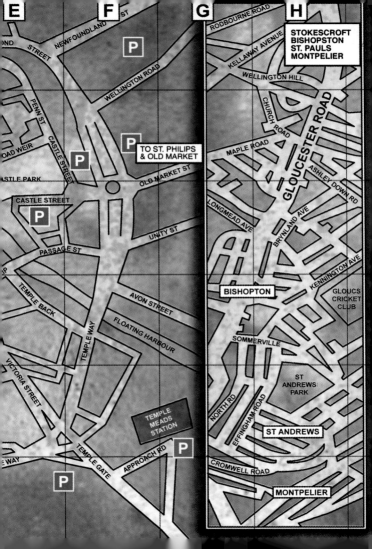

koko.com

BUBBLEGUM
PROMOTIONS

bubblegum

AVAILABLE FOR:
CORPORATE
EVENTS
THEME PARTIES
OR DJ HIRE

CONTACT US ON: 0774 822 3722